THE BRAIN POWER
STORY HOUR

ALSO BY
NANCY J. POLETTE

Brain Power Through Picture Books:
Help Children Develop with Books That Stimulate
Specific Parts of Their Minds (McFarland, 1992)

Books and Real Life:
A Guide for Gifted Students
and Teachers (McFarland, 1984)

THE BRAIN POWER STORY HOUR

Higher Order Thinking with Picture Books

Nancy J. Polette

McFarland & Company, Inc., Publishers
Jefferson, North Carolina, and London

KH

ISBN 0-7864-6853-9

softcover : acid free paper ∞

LIBRARY OF CONGRESS CATALOGUING DATA ARE AVAILABLE

British Library cataloguing data are available

Cover images © 2012 Shutterstock
Front cover design by Bernadette Skok (bskok@ptd.net)

Manufactured in the United States of America

*McFarland & Company, Inc., Publishers
Box 611, Jefferson, North Carolina 28640
www.mcfarlandpub.com*

4/15/13

Acknowledgments

The following publishers have given permission for the use of their catalog copy, internet copy and book jacket copy in the descriptions of titles which are included in *The Brain Power Story Hour.*

Abingdon; Abrams Books; August House; Bethany House Publishers; Bloomsbury U.S.A/Walker; Boyds Mill Press; Candlewick Press; Chicken House Publishers; Children's Press; Marshall Cavandish; Children's Book Press; Chronicle Books; The Creative Company; Crown Publishers; Houghton Mifflin/Clarion; Houghton Mifflin/Harcourt; HarperCollins Children's Book Group, including Greenwillow; Eerdmans Books; Macmillan/Holt; Kingfisher Books; Alfred A. Knopf; Little Brown; Mitten Press; North South Books; Orchard Books; Peachtree; Pelican Books; Penguin Group, including: Coward McCann, Dial, Dutton, G.P. Putnam's Sons, Grosset &Dunlap, Philomel, Phyllis Fogelman Books, Prentice Hall, Puffin Books, Viking; Random House & Random House Imprints; Raven Tree; Roaring Brook; Scholastic and Scholastic Imprints; Shens Books; Simon & Schuster Imprints, including: Aladdin, Atheneum, Margaret McElderry Books, Sleeping Bear Press

Table of Contents

Introduction

When is the story hour more than the sharing of a story? When each story shared leads to the development of productive and critical thinking skills with preschool and primary grade children. These are the years when 80 percent of brain development takes place. The brain power story hour provides a unique opportunity to share books specifically selected to develop the ability to think productively and critically.

While there are many texts available on child development and on planning and implementing a variety of story times in both school and public libraries, there is NO book available that brings together extensive booktalks and follow-up activities specifically designed to build brain power through higher order thinking.

The research of Paul Torrance shows no relationship between students with high academic performance and job success after graduation. While these students could retain and give back information, many were unable to think critically, solve problems and develop new ideas on their own. These skills can be taught in early childhood!

The brain power story hour was successfully developed and became an integral part of the curriculum in the preschool/kindergarten laboratory school of Lindenwood University in St. Charles, Missouri. Ninety percent of the children in this program went on to be selected for gifted programs in both public and private schools.

No special expertise is needed in the sharing of the books and activities in *The Brain Power Story Hour*. Many titles are included for each thinking skill, which allows for a wide range of selection. Each title is followed either by questions to ask and/or activities to develop the skill.

Who Needs This Book?

(1) Children's librarians in public libraries. Adding a higher order thinking skills dimension to the story hour should have great appeal to young parents who want the best programs for their children as shared by professionals.

(2) School librarians who, in working with teachers, can add another level to the story time and at the same time recommend books to be shared in the classroom to develop productive and critical thinking skills.

(3) Teachers of early childhood gifted programs who place great emphasis on higher order thinking and who are eager for materials to promote these thinking skills. Parents, including those who home school, who are looking for professional expertise in helping their children acquire essential thinking skills beyond memorization of facts.

(4) Parents and homeschoolers who want to add a thinking dimension to the sharing of literature.

The Brain Power Story Hour requires no special training to use. Background information, introductory activities for each thinking skill, books and activities that involve the children are ready to use and add a complete and exciting new dimension to the story hour.

ONE

Literacy Versus Letteracy

A major goal in all education programs, including those in early childhood, is to help each child reach an acceptable level of competence in understanding and using language in both oral and written form. Totalitarian governments have long known that taking away books simplifies language and consequently simplifies thought. Programs that stress literacy must be concerned with the development of critical and productive thinking. All free societies value the growth and development of communication skills of their people, yet modern technology, including television, computers and cell phones, has had an adverse effect on the individual's ability to communicate. The average television program provides a ready example of over-simplification of speech, content and theme. The viewing process itself preempts individual communication and eliminates the need (or the desire) for reading and for any form of higher order thinking. Television's common images deaden the imagination and distort reality. Texting on cell phones has created a generation of children who cannot spell.

Unfortunately, in an effort to combat the detrimental effect of the media on the communication skills of young children, many early childhood programs in teaching preliteracy skills (vocabulary, print awareness, letter recognition and phonics) have substituted flash cards and drill for meaningful experiences with literature. Preschool children are exposed to phonics and word drills often before their brains have developed sufficiently to deal with these skills. In her book, *Your Child's Growing Mind*, Dr. Jane Healy cautions that "trying to speed learning over unfinished neural systems can leave permanent damage." Children exposed to such "skill and drill" programs become "letterate" rather than literate. They can pronounce words as unrelated hoops to jump through with little or no understanding of the meaning behind the words.

Knowledge of brain development combined with the research of Ned Herrmann, Bernice McCarthy, Tony Gregorc, Howard Gardner and others on the different thinking modes of the brain provides exciting possibilities for those who work with young children in any capacity, whether the parent, caregiver, teacher or children's librarian. It is exciting to note that these adults, in sharing specially chosen literature followed by brain compatible activities, can help children develop intellectual, contextual and creative brain power to its fullest potential. There is no forced memorization or drill.

Great books do help to shape great minds. Understanding real humanity, nobility of character and the vitality of love through books of quality, rather than having only the plastic manikins of video games and the TV world as models, helps one to live life deeply. Through inspired books, children have an opportunity to know those who live their lives with skill.

Children do not need more and more words bombarding them from all sides. They need deeper, more beautiful, more mind stretching ideas to confront. They need to be offered books with a variety of levels of learning to free their minds of the gymnastics of which they are capable. The deliberate selection of specific types of books can stimulate different areas of the brain, causing growth of neural networks. Those who help young children to start a love affair with books for life are at the same time taking giant steps toward development of higher-level thinking skills essential for daily life.

The idea of whole brain development is based on the fact that as each of the separate thinking skills is called into play, new neural networks form in the part of the brain exercising the skill. Jane Healy, in *Your Child's Growing Mind*, brings together the work of many researchers to explain that during the early years neural networks grow in a child's brain as a result of the mental and physical activities of the child. Every time the young child responds to new sights, sounds, smells, tastes or feelings, new physical connections are formed in the brain. Consequently, the more neural networks or connections the child has, the greater their mental powers and abilities will be. Thus, a wide variety of quality literature must be shared with young children.

Higher Order Thinking

The titles recommended in *The Brain Power Story Hour* are not randomly selected. They are specifically chosen to stimulate mental activity in different parts of the young child's developing brain and to foster those thinking skills essential to successful learning and living.

These skills include:

- Understanding and analyzing fact-based material
- Planning and organizing data and activities
- Mathematical/logical thinking
- Language and linguistic skills
- Feeling-based intrapersonal relationships
- Creativity
- Visual Literacy

THINKING ABILITIES OF THE LEFT AND RIGHT AREAS OF THE BRAIN

Upper Right	**Upper Left**
Creator	*Thinker*
Holistic	Logical
Intuitive	Analytical
Synthesizing	Quantitative
Integrating	Fact-Based
Lower Right	**Lower Left**
Affective	*Organizer*
Emotional	Planned
Interpersonal	Organized
Feeling Based	Detailed
Kinesthetic	Sequential
Relationships	

Thinking Processes of the Left Brain

Note from the diagram that the left side of the brain deals with language development, fact-based material and the ability to plan, organize and solve problems.

Among the excellent picture books that present the real world in all its wonder are many titles by Seymour Simon, including *Animals Nobody Loves* and *Destination Space*, and Jim Murphy's *Call of the Wolves*, Steve Jenkins' concept books, including *Splat, Squeak and Scatter: What Do You Do with a Tail Like This?*, and Greg Tan's math series, including *Math for All Seasons*.

The development of a strong working vocabulary is another function of the left side of the brain. The emphasis on language development is the function of both upper and lower left quadrants. To expand the ability to think, analyze, reason, make connections and see relationships, we must expand the child's language storehouse — those words the child stores in the brain to speak and write with ease.

Language patterns are stored in the brain by hearing them. From ten to twenty exposures are usually needed before a pattern goes into the long term memory and can be used. Words are the tools of our thoughts and experience. All of us respond to the sound of language, the flow of words, the variety of tones and the combinations of signals. Many authors of picture books revel in our language, in its cadences and intricacies. We can join in their fun of playing with words and help the child's ear to delight in the richness of language by sharing aloud many fine books, from the classic *Just So Stories* by Rudyard Kipling to Larry Shles' *Nose Drops* (about a little lost nose that achieves fame by becoming the most famous nose in all history.

The left side of the brain also deals with the efficient use of information. It allows one to plan, organize, sequence information, problem solve and work with details. It is interesting to note that nearly every major psychologist states that the basic key to intellectual growth is the ability to see patterns and relationships. Among many fine picture books that deal with sequencing, grouping, patterns and relationships are Susan Swanson's *House in the Night,* Lauren Thompson's *Apple Pie That Papa Baked* and Mary Ann Hoberman's *All Kinds of Families.* Delightful problem-solving situations arise in Keith Polette's *Isabelle and the Hungry*

Coyote and *Paco and the Giant Chili Plant.* Mysteries by Crosby Bonsall and Eth Clifford which require analysis and attention to detail can be solved by the youngest readers.

When sharing Tim Egan's *Trial of Cardigan Jones*, four-year-olds responded quickly when asked at the end of the story if Cardigan, a moose with big antlers, had stolen Mrs. Brown's pie. In unison they replied NO! These children had analyzed the facts and recognized Cardigan's clumsiness as he knocked over things in the courtroom, including the judge. They assumed correctly that he had accidentally knocked Mrs. Brown's pie off a windowsill and was unaware that he had done so.

Thinking Processes of the Right Brain

In contrast with the left brain, thinking processes (understanding and analyzing fact-based material, planning and organizing data and activities, mathematical/logical thinking and language and linguistic skills), the right side of the brain controls emotions, visual spatial intelligence, relationships, feelings and kinesthetic ability. Development of these skills includes intrapersonal experiences and the ability to think in pictures and to acquire information by creating mental images. Many strong right brain thinkers show a talent for drawing or painting. Since this is the feeling-based quadrant, the child who has had many early childhood experiences in a "warm fuzzy" family is very likely to develop into a warm, feeling-based adult.

Surely one of the greatest needs in the world today is that of resolving human relationships peacefully. Nations find it hard to understand each other, as do their inhabitants. Books about people facing real challenges and having real feelings can help children to understand and empathize with problems and fears we have in common. Books that can evoke real feeling are essential to the literary diet. Such books can benefit the child and ultimately all others who may be touched by that child's life.

There are literally hundreds of books which will stimulate right brain development, including Jan Brett's *Daisy Comes Home* (Daisy, the smallest hen, is picked on by the others), Amy Hest's *The Dog Who Belonged to No One* (a little lost dog and a lonely girl find each other) and Helen Lester's *Hurty Feelings* (Fragility, the hippo, has her feelings so easily hurt that other animals avoid her). For stimulating the visual/ spatial aspects of this quadrant, share the visual experiences in *A Is for Art* by Steven Johnson, *It's Snowing* by Oliver Dunrea, the wonderful journey books of Mitsumasa Anno and the ever popular *I Spy* series by Jean Marzollo.

Right brain development also deals with creative intuitive abilities which allow one to see things in new ways and to create new ideas, new products and/or new ways of doing things. The creator is impulsive, a risk taker, likes change and has little use for order or time. More important, the creator is aware of beauty in their surroundings. Imagination and fantasy are integral to the upper right quadrant and are vital ingredients to a full and rich life. To paraphrase the Russian writer Korni Chukovsky, "without fantasy and imagination there would be a total halt in all areas of human endeavor."

The daily routine of required pursuits tends to squelch the creative brain. Among the many picture books and activities that nurture creative thought are *Stickman* by Julia Donaldson (predict the many uses for a 12-inch stick before chuckling over the adventures of Stickman), *Jack's House* by Karen Biel (guess how many machines it takes to build a house before joining in the repeating phrases) or *The Harvest Knight* by Mercer Mayer (imagine all the dangers a knight of old might face before reading about the Harvest Knight's adventures).

In sharing many of the titles recommended in this book, watch for the child who bursts with sudden laughter at subtle humor when you are reading aloud. Watch for the brimming of tears when compassion for a wounded child or animal is unleashed. Be alert to the spark of recognition underlying the theme of a simple tale. A good piece of literature is not one-way communication. It is the catalyst to facilitate the young child's own source of unfolding thought.

Thinking Skills Defined

Books and activities in *The Brain Power Story Hour* are designed to build the following:

1. The thinking skills of early childhood: conservation, seriation, classification, reversibility.

2. Verbal/Linguistic Thinking: The development of literacy and the effective use of words.

3. Divergent/Creative Thinking: Developing responses that are fluent, flexible, and original.

4. Convergent/Analytical/Mathematical Thinking: Developing logical, deductive reasoning along with problem solving skills.

5. Visual/Spatial Thinking: The ability to observe closely, manipulate shapes mentally and respond to visual images.

6. Evaluative/Critical Thinking: The ability to make decisions and solve problems based on factual, measurable and observable factors.

7. Interpersonal and Intrapersonal Thinking: The ability to discern the moods, feelings and motivations of others as well as understanding the feelings and motivations of one's self.

8. Naturalistic Thinking: Awareness of one's role as a citizen of the planet we all share.

Many activities suggested in *The Brain Power Story Hour* are those that build hemispheric connections, thus requiring stimulation of right and left brain thinking processes. Examples include the following:

Games such as Simon Says that depend on both visual and verbal clues
Putting together items by following directions
Following directions for art projects
Playing charades
Dramatizing scenes from a story read aloud
Describing how to solve a problem
Puppets and dramatic play
Retelling a story in order
Art projects using a variety of media

Books for Ages and Stages

Throughout *The Brain Power Story Hour* a range of ages is suggested for each annotated title. These general guidelines were applied in assigning the appropriate age levels.

NEWBORN TO AGE TWO

This is a time of extremely rapid physical and cognitive development. Attention span is limited and the child is learning basic vocabulary of up to 250 words by age two and is completely self-centered. Board books for babies should have bright colors, large images and simple words. Familiar objects should be featured along with rhythm and rhyme. Books with repeating patterns (dots, stripes, etc.) are important for this age as well as books with high contrast images. Eighteen-month to two-year-olds will enjoy interacting with lift the flap books or touch and feel titles. Appropriate titles include: Dorothy Kunhardt's *Pat the Bunny*, Eric Hill's *Where's Spot?* and Margaret Wise Brown's *Goodnight Moon*.

An abundance of board books is available from a variety of publishers. Ideal for the very young, these books have simple pictures and are small, with rounded corners for safety and slick covers that can be wiped clean. An excellent example is Jan Brett's *The Umbrella Board Book* as, one by one, tree frog, toucan, kinkajou, baby tapir, quetzal, monkey and jaguar crowd into an open, upside down banana umbrella.

AGES THREE, FOUR AND FIVE

Picture books with large, brightly colored illustrations and a simple story line, repetition and predictability speak to the child whose language skills are rapidly developing to more than 3000 words by age five. Curiosity is a major characteristic for this active child, who still has a short attention span. The child shows interest in words, rhymes, nonsense tales and simple folk tales. Stories should be short but rich in language. A child in this age group enjoys stories that deal with their familiar world and where right and wrong are clearly evident. Among the hundreds of appropriate titles are Eric Carle's *Very Hungry Caterpillar* and Bill Martin's *Chicka, Chicka, Boom, Boom*.

AGES SIX AND SEVEN

The children at this age demonstrate an increased attention span and rapid language development and take pride in their developing ability to read and write. Stories should be short but rich in language and can be continued as chapter books. Informational books can be introduced to satisfy the desire to learn about the world. A sense of humor is developing and children this age like funny books. They can generally distinguish fantasy from reality and they enjoy fantasy tales. Although beginning to develop empathy for others, they value independence and like books about independent characters like Curious George; but they also value books about warm family relationships.

Appropriate titles include the Frog and Toad series by Arnold Lobel and fantasy titles like William Steig's *Doctor DeSoto* and Charlotte Huck's *Princess Furball.*

Helping librarians, teachers, parents and caregivers develop young children's brain power to its fullest potential is the purpose of *The Brain Power Story Hour*: help with selecting books and activities to stimulate thinking in the intellectual, contextual and creative realms; help with selection of the finest books available in children's literature, and help in building warm adult/child relationships through the sharing of wonderful picture books — yardsticks upon which the child will unconsciously measure what is worthy against what is trivial.

References

Cline, Foster. *What Shall We Do with This Kid?* Evergreen Consultants, 1979.
Healy, Jane. *Your Child's Growing Mind.* Doubleday, 2010.
Herrmann, Ned. *The Creative Brain.* Applied Creative Services, 1985.

Picture Books

Biel, Karen. *Jack's House.* Holiday House, 2008.
Brett, Jan. *Daisy Comes Home.* G.P. Putnam's Sons, 2002.
Carle, Eric. *The Very Hungry Caterpillar.* Philomel, 1969.
Donaldson, Julia. *Stick Man.* Scholastic, 2009.
Dunrea, Olivier. *It's Snowing.* Farrar, 2002.
Egan, Tim. *The Trial of Cardigan Jones.* Houghton Mifflin, 2003.
Hest, Amy. *The Dog Who Belonged to No One.* Abrams, 2008.
Hoberman, Mary Ann. *All Kinds of Families,* Little Brown, 2009.

Huck, Charlotte. *Princess Furball.* Greenwillow, 1989.

Jenkins, Steve. *Splat, Squeak and Scatter: What Do You Do with a Tail Like This?* Houghton Mifflin, 2001.

Johnson, Steven. *A Is for Art.* Simon & Schuster, 2008.

Lester, Helen. *Hurty Feelings.* Houghton Mifflin, 2005.

Mayer, Mercer. *The Harvest Knight.* Dial, 2007.

Murphy, Jim. *Call of the Wolves.* Scholastic, 1999.

Polette, Keith. *Isabelle and the Hungry Coyote.* Raven Tree, 2004.

Polette, Keith. *Paco and the Giant Chili Plant.* Raven Tree, 2006.

Simon, Seymour. *Animals Nobody Loves.* SeaStar, 2001.

Simon, Seymour. *Destination Space.* HarperCollins, 2006.

Steig, William. *Doctor DeSoto.* Farrar, Straus & Giroux, 1990.

Swanson, Susan. *The House in the Night.* Houghton Mifflin, 2008.

Tan, Greg. *Math for All Seasons.* Scholastic, 2005.

Thompson, Lauren. *The Apple Pie That Papa Baked.* Simon & Schuster, 2007.

Two

Before We Read

The Work of Jean Piaget

Perhaps more than any single person, Jean Piaget ranks as the giant of contemporary research into the way in which young children's thinking develops. His demonstrations that learning in young children is creative, developmental and an essential part of living and growing have profound implications for early childhood programs.

The development of the child's brain to its fullest potential is an awesome responsibility for those who daily touch children's lives. Yet, there is no greater satisfaction than to have helped a child discover his feelings, new ways of thinking and, ultimately, new worlds.

Piaget theorized that many thinking tasks depend on the child's developmental timetable and that, just as children grow physically at different rates, they grow cognitively at different rates. Some children, for example, read fluently at age four, others not until age eight and, as Piaget discovered, those of exceptional intellectual ability are not necessarily early readers.

Current brain research tells us that Piaget was right. The newborn can see and hear almost at once because the lobes in the brain responsible for those functions are closest to the top of the spine. Until prefrontal lobes (located the greatest distance from the top of the spine), which control the ability to read, fully develop the child is not ready read. This is developmental and has nothing to do with IQ. This complete development takes place somewhere between the ages of four and eight. Thus, trying to speed learning over immature neuron systems is the same as expecting a child who has never had a piano lesson to play a Mozart concerto.

This chapter discusses the early childhood thinking processes of conservation, seriation, classification and reversibility.

Conservation

Conservation is the ability to understand that, as long as nothing is added or taken away, an object will remain the same even though the container, shape, size or position may be altered. The child's ability to understand these concepts generally occurs between the ages of four and eight and includes the following:

1. Conservation of liquids: Understanding that the shape of a container does not change the quantity of liquid poured from one container to another.

2. Conservation of weight: Understanding that weight does not change if the shape of an object changes.

3. Conservation of number: Understanding that the number of objects does not change whether arranged in a row, a circle or any other configuration.

4. Conservation of length: Understanding that two objects of the same length remain the same length whether bent or straight.

The child who has not yet gained an understanding of conservation will see fifty-two letters in the alphabet. She may know the word "Mother" one day because it is the first word in a sentence and begins with an uppercase *M*. She may not recognize the same word the next day if it appears elsewhere in the sentence and begins with a lowercase *m*. Several simple tasks can determine the child's ability to conserve:

1. Use two glasses of approximately the same circumference, one short and the other tall and slender. Fill one-half of the short glass with water. Pour the water into the tall glass (it will rise to a higher level). The child who does not recognize that each glass held the same amount of water is not yet conserving.

2. Show the child two balls of clay of the same size and weight. Ask the child which has more clay. The answer should be that they are the same. Take one ball of clay and role it out in the form of a snake. Now ask the child which has more clay. The child who is not yet conserving will generally point to the snake.

ACTIVITIES FOR CONSERVATION

Herve Tullet. *Press Here*. Chronicle Books, 2010.

Press the yellow dot on the cover of the book and embark on a magical journey. Each page instructs the reader to press the dots (there are fifteen), shake the pages, and tilt the book. Watch the dots multiply and change direction and size, yet when the adventure is complete there are still fifteen dots.

1. Place ten pennies in a row on a flat surface. Ask the child to arrange the pennies in a different way. Are there still ten pennies? Rearrange again. Are there still ten pennies?

2. Use a ball of clay and encourage the child to create a different object (other than the ball shape). Ask: Did we add any clay? Did we take away any clay? Do we still have the same amount of clay?

3. Place two different pictures of the same farm animal on cards, two each of horses, cows, pigs, chickens, lambs, dogs, cats, pigs. Children take turns picking two cards. If they get a match they keep the cards. If not, they return the cards to the pile. The child with the most cards when all cards have been picked is the winner.

BOOKS TO SHARE AND QUESTIONS TO ASK

Bardhan-Quallen, Sudipta. *The Hog Prince*. Illustrated by Jason Wolff. Dutton, 2009. Ages 3–5.

When he learns from a mixed-up fairy godmother that his true love's kiss will transform him from dirty hog to pampered prince, Eldon smooches anyone in sight. But what if true love has been waiting under his snout all along? Ask: No matter where he goes or who he kisses will Eldon still be a hog?

Make a three-sentence pig story. Cut the sentences apart and ask a friend to put them together to tell the story. Can you tell this story?:

His mother scrubbed him clean.
The little pig fell in a mud puddle.
One day a little pig went for a walk.

Brown, Margaret Wise. *The Runaway Bunny*. Illustrated by Clement Hurd. Harper & Row, 1942. Ages 2–4.

A little bunny keeps running away from his mother in an imaginary game of verbal hide-and-seek, pretending to be a fish, a bird or a rock but always remaining the same little bunny his mother loves. How do you know the little bunny is pretending to be something else?

DiCamillo, Kate. *Mercy Watson: Princess in Disguise*. Illustrated by Chris Van Dusen. Candlewick, 2010. Ages 4–6.

When the Watsons decide to zip their pet pig into a form-fitting princess dress and tiara for Halloween, they are certain that Mercy, the pig, will be beautiful beyond compare. Mercy is equally certain she likes the sound of trick-or-treating and can picture piles of buttered toast already. Ask: Is a pig still a pig even disguised as a princess?

Trick or Treating Game: The leader says, "I am going trick or treating and I hope someone will give me butter. You can come with me if you can think of something that begins with the letter *B*." The child who can name something that begins with the letter *B* can continue the game as the leader uses a different letter.

Donaldson, Julia. *Stick Man*. Illustrated by Axel Scheffler. Scholastic, 2009. Ages 3–5.

Stick Man lives in the family tree with his Stick Lady Love and their stick children three. But one day, Stick Man is carried off by a mischievous dog who wants to play fetch! Things go from bad to worse as Stick Man is carried farther and farther away from home. Lonely and lost, Stick Man desperately wants to get home to be with his family for Christmas but finds himself in a fireplace. On Christmas Eve, who do you suppose will rescue him before the fire is lit? Is he still a stickman in the water? As the castle flag? In the fireplace? How do you know? Students brainstorm as many uses as they can for a 12-

inch stick. All answers are accepted. Generally speaking, the most creative responses will come last.

Flaherty, Alice. *Luck of the Loch Ness Monster.* Illustrated by Scott Magoon. Houghton Mifflin, 2007. Ages 4–6.

On an ocean trip, a little girl named Katrina-Elizabeth tosses her oatmeal overboard because oatmeal is her least favorite food. A small worm swims alongside the ocean liner eating bowl after bowl of tossed oatmeal. He has never tasted anything as wonderful as oatmeal in his whole life. Is the huge monster at the end of the story the same little worm that began the long swim? How do you know? Encourage children as a group to complete the sea monster description that follows:

FLASH! A sea monster was sighted yesterday by Dr. Brown, who felt _____at the sight of the creature and described him as being ____ feet tall and weighing _____pounds. He was the color of _____. His head was _____and his body was _____ and he smelled a little like _____. Anyone seeing this creature should beware because it might _____anyone it catches.

Gravett, Emily. *Blue Chameleon.* Simon & Schuster, 2010. Ages 3–6.

The lonely blue chameleon tries to fit in by changing color and shape but no one wants to be his friend. As the chameleon changes shape and color is he still the same chameleon? Just as the chameleon changed his color, so we can change a word by changing a letter. Ask: How can we make new words from dig by changing the first letter?

Joffe, Laura Numeroff. *Why a Disguise?* Illustrated by David McPhail. Aladdin Books, 1999. Ages 3–5.

There are times in life when it's useful for a kid to assume a new identity — especially when it's their turn at the dentist's office or Mom is serving lima beans or the class bully is waiting for them after school. Yet, is it the same little boy underneath the mask, the glasses and the beard? Play animal disguise. A bat grows whiskers and a tail and becomes a _____ (cat). A dog turns into a piece of wood and becomes a ____ (log). A cow says "oink" and becomes a ____ (sow).

Kerby, Johanna. *Little Pink Pup.* G.P. Putnam's Sons, 2010. Ages 2–4.

When Pink's siblings push him out of the way, the little pig finds a mother dog who welcomes him. Even though little pink pig is not in the place he *should* be, is he still a little pink pig? Pink and pig have the same beginning letters. Ask the child to name other farm animals and describe them by using the same beginning letters (hairy horse, lazy lamb, chunky chicken, heavy hog, etc.).

Marzollo, Jean. *Pretend You're a Cat*. Illustrated By Jerry Pinkney. Puffin Books, 2000. Ages 2–4.

In this book of rhyming verse and full-color illustrations, young readers are asked to use their imagination to transform themselves into a full cast of animals, such as a fish, bird, cow or cat. Allow the child plenty of time to role-play the animal he wishes to be. Ask: No matter which you pretend to be, are you still you?

Have the child create cat riddles with rhyming words. Example: What do you call a cat that wears something on its head? A hat cat.

McKee, David. *Elmer*. HarperCollins, 1989. Ages 3–5.

Elmer the elephant is bright-colored patchwork all over. No wonder the other elephants laugh at him! If he were ordinary elephant color, the others might stop laughing. Ask: That would make Elmer feel better, wouldn't it? Even though he changes his color to grey, Elmer remains the same lovable elephant. Pair this book with nonfiction picture books about animals that change color. See how many ways can children finish this sentence: An elephant would be a wonderful friend because.

Pelley, Kathleen. *Magnus Maximus, a Marvelous Measurer*. Illustrated by S.D. Schindler. Farrar, 2010. Ages 4–6.

Magnus Maximus is a marvelous measurer. He measures wetness and dryness and nearness and farness, and everything in between. When a lion escapes from a traveling circus, Magnus and his trusty measuring tape come to the rescue. Now a hero, all is well until the day Magnus accidentally breaks his glasses, and he sees — for the first time — that he's been missing out on life's simple pleasures. Ask: What can you use to measure things? What things can you measure? Let children guess how many inches of string it would take to go around a jar or a pumpkin or another object, then measure with a piece of string to support or deny estimates.

Weber, Belinda. *Animal Disguises*. Kingfisher, 2007 Ages 4–6.

Investigate the exciting world of animal camouflage. Discover how creatures blend in with their environment. Ask: Does mimicking leaves, stones, and flowers, playing tricks on their predators, and changing shape create a different animal or the same animal? How do you know?

Play the animal guessing game:

What animal is the color of grass? Its name rhymes with "gizzard" (lizard).

What animal's coat is the color of snow? Its name rhymes with "hair" (polar bear).

What animal's coat is the color of sand? Its name rhymes with "log" (prairie dog).

Zane, Alexander. *The Wheels on the Race Car*. Illustrated by James Warhola. Orchard Books, 2005. Ages 3–5.

"Racers, start your engines! The drivers in the race car yell, 'Go, go, go!'" Here at the racetrack, animals are busy from start to finish zipping, zooming, and zizzing. See if you can keep up with these dare-devils and their fans as they race to the finish line. Ask: No matter where they are or what changes are made, are these the same race cars that began the race? Take an ABC ride. Ask: What might the race car drive past that begins with each letter of the alphabet? (Eliminate X and Z.)

Example: A=ambulance, B=billboard, etc.

Seriation

Seriation is the ability to arrange similar objects according to some dimension, such as weight, size, color, shape, or type. As children's brains develop, so does their ability to see order. Given a group of objects and asked to place them in order from smallest to largest, the four-year-old should easily be able to accomplish the task, while the three-year-old may have difficulty with the same task. It is important to note that, while these early childhood thinking processes tend to develop at certain ages, the rate of development can vary widely from child to child.

Many mathematical concepts depend on the ability to recognize order, such as largest to smallest, more or less, greater than or less than — all important seriation skills. These same skills come into play with higher-order thinking and problem solving. To determine order, all objects must be analyzed before order can be achieved. Seriation skills can be introduced with both hands-on activities (for example, placing a variety of different books in order from smallest to largest) and more abstract activities — retelling story events in order.

ACTIVITIES FOR SERIATION

1. Recalling Story Order: Share any picture book that features more than one animal.

Share this song after reading about animals found in a particular place (forest, desert, arctic region, mountain, jungle). Sing to the tune of "The Bear Went Over the Mountain":

When we first hiked in the _____ (forest, desert, mountain, jungle),
When we first hiked in the _____ (forest, desert, mountain, jungle),
When we first hiked in the _____ (forest, desert, mountain, jungle),
What do you think we saw?
We saw a _____ in the _____,
We saw a _____ in the _____,
We saw a _____ in the _____,
A _____ is what we saw.

Continue with naming the animals in the story in order, using the following:

When we next hiked in the _____ (forest, desert, mountain, jungle),
When we next hiked in the _____ (forest, desert, mountain, jungle),

When we next hiked in the _____ *(forest, desert,*
    mountain, jungle),
What do you think we saw?

2. Recalling Character Order

Example: Allen, Pamela. *Who Sank the Boat?* Coward McCann, 1985. Ages 3–5.

In a small house by the river live a number of animals. One day they decide to get in a very small rowboat. As each animal steps in, the boat sinks lower and lower. Finally, when the last animal — a mouse — jumps in, the boat sinks.

Add more verses to introduce the animals in the order they appear in the story

    A _____ jumped in the boat.
    A _____ jumped in the boat.
    A _____ jumped in the boat.
    Look and see —
    One, two, three.
    A _____ jumped in the boat.

Use the same pattern for other stories and characters. Change the verb and prepositional phrase to fit the story.

Example: *Share Corduroy* by Don Freeman

    The toy was on the shelf.
    The girl waked in the store.
    The guard looked at the bear.

3. ABC Order

Each child can become a character in the story that has been shared. Children line up in alphabetical order by the characters' names.

4. Password

The leader names an animal in the story (e.g., a mule). The first child to give a word that rhymes with mule can pass through the magic path (walk in a circle around a chair or desk).

5. Counting Rhymes

Use animals or characters from a story for the spaces in this rhyme. Animals or characters are added in the order in which they appear in the story.

Five (big, little, brave, etc.) _____ coming in the door —
One (walked, ran, etc.) away
And then there were four.
Four (big, little, brave, etc.) _____ looking at me —
One (walked, swam, ran, etc.) away
And then there were three.
Three (big, little, brave, etc.) _____ looking at you —
One (walked, swam, ran, etc.) away
And then there were two
Two (big, little, brave, etc.) _____ having lots of fun —
One (walked, swam, ran, etc.) away
And then there was one
One (big, little, brave, etc.) _____ sitting in the sun —
The moon came out
And then there were none.

COUNTING FOR SPRING

One little raindrop falling through the air,
Two little raindrops falling here and there.
Three busy robins hopping all around,
Looking for a juicy worm hiding in the ground.
Four big woodpeckers tapping on the trees,
Look out! Here come five bumblebees.
Six ladybugs crawling up a wall,
Seven roosters crowing a morning wake-up call.
Eight pink tulips bending in the breeze,
The old dog scratches nine pesky fleas.
Ten children outside, playing tag and then,
They look up high and see the sun,
Spring is here again!

BOOKS TO SHARE AND QUESTIONS TO ASK

Beaumont, Karen. *No Sleep for the Sheep*. Illustrated by Jackie Urbanovic. Houghton Mifflin, 2011. Ages 2–4.

One tired sheep wants nothing more than a good night's sleep. All is peaceful until a duck arrives at the barn door followed by a goat, a pig, a cow and a horse, each larger and louder than the last. Let children take the animal parts and make the animal sounds as they appear, in the right order. When all appear let them make their sounds together. The leader then says, "My, what a noisy barnyard!"

Carle, Eric. *The Very Hungry Caterpillar.* Philomel, 1981. Ages 3–5.

A small caterpillar eats through a variety of foods, increasing the amounts each day from Monday to Saturday. After eating a green leaf for an upset stomach he begins the process to become a butterfly.

Sing to the tune of "I'm a Little Teapot":

> *Look at the butterfly*
> *That grew from a caterpillar,*
> *Slowly, slowly from a caterpillar.*
> *In the chrysalis it grew and grew.*
> *Look at the butterfly.*
> *It's looking at you.*

Cronin, Doreen. *Diary of a Worm.* Illustrated by Harry Bliss. HarperCollins, 2003. Ages 3–5.

This is the diary of a worm not that different from you or me. Except he eats his homework. Oh, and his head looks a lot like his rear end. Follow his life for a day from beginning to end. Ask the listeners to recall each event in order and list things worm did in the story (dug tunnels, taught spider).

Put two of the things you listed on the lines in the song below (sing to the tune of *London Bridge*):

> *Wiggly worm dug tunnels, dug tunnels, dug tunnels,*
> *Wiggly worm dug tunnels and taught spider.*

dePaola, Tomi. *Strega Nona's Harvest.* G.P. Putnam's Sons, 2009. Ages 3–5.

Strega Nona attempts to teach Big Anthony about gardening and the importance of order. But when Big Anthony does not follow her directions and tries to use her growing spell, his small vegetable patch turns into an unruly jungle! What will they do with all the extra vegetables? Ask: Why is following directions important?

Play the clue game. Guess the activity. Read the clues in order, allowing time for children to guess after each clue is read. The answer is "planting a garden."

1. You can do it alone.
2. You usually handle more than one item when you do it.
3. You can do it just for yourself.
4. Its name rhymes with "pardon."
5. A hoe and a spade are needed to do it.

Fleming, Candace. *Gator Gumbo*. Illustrated by Sally Anne Lambert. Farrar, 2004. Ages 3–5.

Poor Monsieur Gator is moving so slowly he can't catch himself a taste of possum. Day after day other animals tease and taunt him, until, finally, he decides to cook up some gumbo. But who will help him boil, catch, sprinkle, and chop? Certainly not rude Ms. Possum, ornery Mr. Otter, or sassy Ms. Skunk. But when the gumbo is ready and they want to eat it, they are in for a big surprise. List the steps in making the gumbo. Suppose Mr. Otter added something to the gumbo that begins with the letter *O*. What could it be?

Franco, Betsy. *Pond Circle*. Illustrated by Stefano Vitale. McElderry Books, 2009. Ages 2–4.

One summer night by a small pond, mayflies dart, beetles dive, frogs spring, skunks shuffle, and owls swoop. As a young girl watches, the circle of life unfolds. Draw the creatures in the order they appeared in the book. Share this poem, with the children repeating each line after you:

THE POND

Moon glows, dark pond,
Turtles creep, quiet pond.
Fish rest, still pond,
Snakes hiss, slithery pond.
Fireflies glow, light pond,
Mosquitoes whine, goodnight pond!

Paul, Ann. *Manana Iguana*. Illustrated by Ethan Long. Holiday House, 2004. Ages 3–5.

This is a Hispanic version of *The Little Red Hen*. Iguana is planning a fiesta. Tortuga the tortoise, Gonejo the rabbit, and Gulebra the snake all want to come. But they do not want to help Iguana deliver invitations or stuff the pinata or cook the food. Iguana must do all of the tasks alone. Ask: If you could take away any one task that Iguana did, could Iguana still have the party? Why or why not?

Potter, Beatrix. *The Tale of Peter Rabbit*. Warne, 1866. Ages 2–4.

Young Peter, hungry for cabbages and carrots, explores forbidden territory in Mr. McGregor's garden. When Peter is discovered he is chased from a watering can, past the potting shed, the onions, a cat and a mouse before finding the safety of home. As children listen to the story, ask them to draw a map of Peter's travels.

Robart, Rose. *The Cake That Mack Ate*. Illustrated by Maryann Kovalski. Little, Brown, 1988. Ages 2–4.

Here is the cake that Mack ate. Here is the hen that laid the egg that went into the cake that Mack ate. As each ingredient is added and including the farmer who grew the seed and the woman who married the farmer, we finally meet Mack, a playful dog who ate the cake. Draw and cut apart pictures of a hen, an egg, some corn, a farmer, his wife and some candles. Ask children to arrange the pictures in the order they appeared in the story.

Rosen, Michael. *We're Going on a Bear Hunt*. McElderry, 2009. Ages 2–5.

Have you ever gone on a bear hunt? Come along on this one with a brave young family — four children (including the baby) and their father. They're not scared. With them you will cross a field of tall, wavy grass ("Swishy swashy!"), wade through a deep, cold river ("Splash splosh!"), struggle through swampy mud ("Squelch squelch!"), find your way through a big, dark forest ("Stumble trip!"), fight through a whirling snowstorm ("Hoooo woooo!"), and enter a narrow, gloomy cave. what's that? You'll soon learn just what to do to escape from a big, furry bear. Encourage children to act out the bear hunt.

Stevens, Janet. *The Little Red Pen*. Illustrated by Susan Stevens Crummel. Houghton Mifflin, 2011. Ages 4–6.

Poor Little Red Pen! She can't possibly correct a mountain of homework all by herself. Who will help her? "Not I!" says Stapler. "Not I!"
says Eraser. "Yo no!" says Pushpin. But when the Little Red Pen tum-
bles in exhaustion into the Pit of No Return (the trash!), her fellow
school supplies must work together to rescue her. Trouble is, their
plan depends on Tank, the class hamster, who's not inclined to coop-
erate. Will the Little Red Pen be lost forever?

Sturges, Philomon. *She'll Be Comin' Round the Mountain When She
Comes.* Illustrated by Ashley Wolff. Little, Brown, 2004. Ages
4–6.

A Hispanic version in which a community of southwestern animals,
including a coyote, lizard, armadillo, wren, possum, and raccoon,
scurry about to prepare for the arrival of a mysterious guest. As the
anticipation and excitement build, they all begin to wonder what "she"
will be like. The discovery of her identity proves to be a javelina with
a bookmobile! Ask: What did the animals do first? second? last? Ask
children to add their favorite subjects to the verse below (sing to the
tune "She'll Be Comin' Round the Mountain"):

Here's a book about a _____just for you.
Here's a book about a _____just for you.
Here's a book about a _____.
Here's a book about a _____.
Here's a book about a _____just for you.

Swanson, Susan. *The House in the Night.* Illustrated by Beth
Krommes. Houghton Mifflin, 2008. Ages 2–4.

Here we find light coming from the windows of the house in the
night and as we enter the house we find nighttime things: a key, a bed,
a book, the moon and other items familiar to the young child. Ask:
Would these items need to be put in any special order? Why or why
not? Suppose instead of these items we found an item that rhymes
with each. What might we find?

Key: tree, bee, flea, me, pea, tea,
Bed: bread, head, sled
Book: hook, cook, crook
Moon: loon, spoon, tune, prune

Thompson, Lauren. *The Apple Pie That Papa Baked.* Illustrated by Jonathan Bean. Simon & Schuster, 2007. Ages 3–5.

These are the apples, juicy and red, that went in the pie, warm and sweet, that Papa baked — for guess who! This is a cumulative tale. Ask: Does it make any difference the order in which the ingredients go into the apple pie? Why or why not?

Share this poem. Encourage children to join in when they see the pattern:

> Mother in the kitchen on a sunny day.
> Time to cook, No time to play.
> Father in the kitchen on a sunny day.
> Time to cook, No time to play.
> Sister in the kitchen on a sunny day.
> Time to cook, No time to play.
> Brother the kitchen on a sunny day.
> Time to cook, No time to play.
> Grandma in the kitchen on a sunny day.
> Time to cook, No time to play
> Family in the kitchen, tell me why.
> They're cooking up an apple pie!

Viorst, Judith. *Alexander and the Terrible, Horrible, No Good, Very Bad Day.* Simon & Schuster, 1972. Ages 4–6.

Alexander goes to sleep with gum in his mouth and wakes up with gum in his hair. When he gets out of bed, he trips over his skateboard and by mistake drops his sweater in the sink while the water is running. He can tell it is going to be a terrible, horrible, no good, very bad day. Nothing at all is right. Everything goes wrong, right down to lima beans for supper and kissing on TV. What do you do on a day like that? Well, you may think about going to Australia. Assign roles to the children: gum, pajamas, cereal box, car, skateboard, sweater, tooth, lima beans, TV. Challenge the children to line up in the order the items (gum, skateboard, sweater, cereal box, car, etc.) appeared in the story.

Play the Alphabet Game: Students choose how many letters they want to say in order to be the first person to say Z. For example, if one student chooses 4 that student will begin by saying A, B, C, D. If the next student chooses 3 that student will say E, F, G. The game continues with each student giving in turn the number of letter they chose.

Ward, Cindy. *Cookie's Week*. G.P. Putnam's Sons, 1988. Ages 2–4.

Cookie the cat gets into trouble each day of the week, finally resting on Sunday. As she explores places she isn't supposed to be she leaves a mess behind her. Recall where Cookie went each day of the week. Suppose Cookie went to school. Ask: What kind of trouble might she get into there?

> On Monday Cookie got into the waste can.
> There was _____ everywhere.
> On Tuesday Cookie got into the fishbowl.
> There was _____ everywhere.
> On Wednesday Cookie got into the _____.
> There was _____ everywhere.
> On Thursday Cookie got into the _____.
> There was _____ everywhere.
> On Friday Cookie got into the _____.
> There was _____ everywhere.
> Today is Saturday. Maybe Cookie will _____.

Classification

Classification is the ability to group within categories. Young children tend to identify objects in a group by function. ("You eat with these. You play with these.") As neuron systems mature, the child will begin to group by other attributes (things made of paper, round things, etc.). Classification, which requires the identification of specific attributes in order to place items in categories, is essential to both concept and vocabulary development. Preschool children learn to classify with sorting activities using actual objects. Primary children can be challenged to group pictures of objects cut from magazines. Classification can be done by weight, number, length, size or similar attributes.

ACTIVITIES FOR CLASSIFICATION

1. Sorting

Gather a collection of nonfiction books — four each about animals, machines, objects, flowers, vegetables and fruits. Demonstrate the sorting activity by sorting into two sets (for example, four flowers and four machines). Say: "I have sorted my books into those about flowers and those about machines What other ways might I sort the books?"

Allow the children time to sort. Can they find two groups of items? Complete these sentences:

These books are about _____.

These books are not about _____.

All books can then be put back in the pile and the child/ren are encouraged to sort in a different way, perhaps by size or shape.

2. A Grouping Game

Let the children form a circle. Name a category, for example, Animals. Pull five names from a box, one at a time. If the child whose name is called can name a story with an animal in it they go to the center of the circle. Explain that the circle is the library and the stories in the center are the books. Play the game several times so that each child's name is called. Other categories can arise from the book that is shared. Examples follow:

Book	***Category***
Fairy Tale News from Hidden Forest	Fairy tale characters
Now Hiring: White House Dog	Pets
Only One Neighborhood	Stores or businesses
Way Far Away on a Wild Safari	Wild animals
Which Shoes Will You Choose?	Clothing
Winter Is the Warmest Season	Things associated with a
The Cow Loves Cookies	season
	Desserts

3. Singing

Choose a category such as fairy tale characters. Name characters that belong in that group (Princess, Prince, King, Queen, Giant, Witch, etc.). Sing to "There's a Hole in the Bottom of the Sea":

There's a princess in the middle of the book,
There's a princess in the middle of the book,
There's a princess,
There's a princess,
There's a princess in the middle of the book.
There's a prince by the princess in the middle of the book.
There's a king by the prince by the princess in the middle of the book.
There's a queen by the king by the prince by the princess in the middle of the book.
Add more characters.

4. Sharing Animal Stories.

Display books about a variety of animals. Include birds, mammals, reptiles, farm animals, pets, and wild animals. Challenge the child/ren to find two alike and one different and orally complete these sentences:

A (*cat*) has (*fur*).
A (*dog*) has (*fur*).
A (*frog*) does not have (*fur*).

5. Fairy Tale Classification Activities

After sharing:	*Name:*
Red Riding Hood	Things found in a forest. Things not found in a forest.
Snow White	Things found in a castle. Things not found in a castle.
Three Little Pigs	These are farm animals. These are not farm animals.
The Three Bears	These are wild animals. These are not wild animals.
Rapunzel	These grow in a vegetable garden. These do not grow in a vegetable garden.
Little Red Hen	These are needed for baking bread. These are not needed for baking bread.

6. Chanting: Choose a Topic (such as Winter)

Each child will name and give a one-word description of something associated with winter then say their item and description when the leader points to them. Example:

WINTER THINGS!

White snow	Cold winds
Clear ice	Smoky chimneys
Sparkling sleet	Fast sleds

These are just a few. Name and describe seven more things associated with winter.

Colored scarves	Warm fires
Fuzzy mittens	Hot chocolate
Heavy coats	Wool sweaters, too
Rubber boots	

From near and far
Here they are
WINTER THINGS!

BOOKS TO SHARE AND QUESTIONS TO ASK

Ada, Alma Flor. *Extra! Extra! Fairy Tale News from Hidden Forest.* Illustrated by Leslie Tryon. Atheneum, 2007. Ages 4–7.

An enormous beanstalk has sprouted outside Jack's house. Hare and Tortoise are off to the races. Fairy tale characters are making headlines. Name many fairy tale characters. Ask: How might you group the characters you named? Suppose you read some want ads by fairy tale characters. Who might place a want ad for (1) a glass slipper (2) magic beans (3) a gingerbread house (4) a person to repair chairs (5) sticks, straw and bricks (6) a comb and brush. Answer key: (1) Cinderella (2) Jack (3) Hansel & Gretel (4) Baby Bear (5) Three Pigs (6) Rapunzel

Alsenas, Linas. *Peanut.* Scholastic, 2007. Ages 4–6.

Lonely Mildred finds a pet she thinks is a dog, but it doesn't act at all as a dog should. It is gray and has a long trunk. This is a fun story and a good writing model. Give three clues that describe an animal that is usually a pet. Ask others to name the pet and tell in what group it belongs (dogs, cats, etc.), for example: (1) It has four legs, (2) It is covered with fur, (3) Its name rhymes with fog.

Arnosky, Jim. *I'm a Turkey!* Scholastic, 2009. Ages 3–5.

Learn fun turkey facts with Tom the Turkey and his flock, who are always on the lookout for hungry animals. Name and group as many birds as you can. Possible groupings might be by size, color, winter and summer birds, etc.

Draw and color a turkey. Spread out your fingers, Draw around your open hand. Your thumb is the turkey's head, your fingers are the feathers.

Ashburn, Boni. *Over at the Castle.* Illustrated by Kelly Murphy. Abrams, 2010. Ages 4–6.

Here is a delightful counting book that introduces all of the workers in a castle watched over by two eager dragons. After sharing the book ask the children to name some jobs today that would not be done in a castle. See how many ways can children complete this paragraph.

The important thing about a castle is _____.

It _____.

And it _____.

And sometimes _____.

But the important thing about a castle is _____.

Brown, Margaret Wise. *Goodnight Moon.* Illustrated by Clement Hurd. Harper & Row, 1947. Ages 2–4.

In a great green room, tucked away in bed, is a little bunny. "Goodnight room, goodnight moon." And to all the familiar things in the softly lit room — to the picture of the three little bears sitting on chairs, to the clocks and his socks, to the mittens and the kittens, to everything one by one — the little bunny says goodnight. Ask children to name another room in their house. To what objects in a kitchen might we say "Good Morning"? (Tune: "The Bear Went Over the Mountain"):

> *Who do we wish a good morning?*
> *Who do we wish a good morning?*
> *Who do we wish a good morning?*
> *It's a word that rhymes with late (plate).*

Add more verses using kitchen objects.

Donaldson, Julia. *Where's My Mom?* Illustrated by Axel Scheffler. Dial, 2008. Ages 3–5.

When little monkey can't find his mother, butterfly offers to help in the search. Little monkey says that his mother is big, so butterfly leads him to an elephant. Little monkey says his mom is furry, so butterfly leads him to a bat. From then on, little monkey and butterfly meet many jungle animals, but they don't find Mom until little monkey comes up with just the right description. List all the ways animals might be grouped (big, little, with fur, feathers, etc.). Name two animals that belong in each group. Sing about each animal in the story using this pattern. (Tune: "Did You Ever See a Lassie?"). Name each animal and tell how it moves.

> *Did you ever see a monkey, a monkey, a monkey?*
> *Did you ever see a monkey swing this way and that?*
> *Swing this way and that way, Swing this way and that way.*
> *Did you ever see a monkey swing this way and that?*

Harshman, Marc. *Only One Neighborhood.* Illustrated by Barbara Garrison Dutton, 2007. Ages 4–6.

One bakery has many different breads; in one school there are many children. This unique book uses a busy city neighborhood to teach the concept of one versus many. Only One Neighborhood takes children on a tour of shops, the firehouse, and more. At the book's end, readers see how many neighborhoods can come together to make one city, showing how each one of us is part of something bigger. Name other parts that when put together make a whole.

Play the ABC Seller Game: One child begins with "In my city there is an Apple seller." The next child mentions a business that begins with B (perhaps Beauty Shop). Let the group help those who cannot think of a product or business for a particular letter. Skip letters *X* and *Z*.

Hughes, Shirley. *Bathwater's Hot.* Walker, 2001 Ages 2–4.

A nursery picture book, featuring a lively toddler and her baby brother, it is designed to introduce concepts such as opposites, colors, sounds, shapes and sizes to young children. How many sentences can children complete?

Oral activity: A _____ is hot but a _____ is cold. Make sentences for tall/short. night/day, sweet/sour, and add other opposites the children suggest.

Jocelyn, Marthe. *Hanna's Collections.* Dutton, 2000. Ages 3–5.

Hannah loves to make collections. Whether it's new barrettes for her hair or seashells from the shore, she likes to gather things and sort them by size, shape, and color. But now she is facing a problem. The children in her class have been invited to bring their favorite collection to school. How can she possibly pick a favorite? She finds a way to show off all of her collections in a surprising new way. What are some fun things you might collect?

Give each child a card with a picture of something one might collect: stamps, coins, flowers, salt shakers, toy cars, fans, hats, rocks, books, etc. The leader calls out: "Coins change places with fans." "It" tries to get to fans' seat before "coins" gets there.

Kirk, Daniel. *Library Mouse a World to Explore.* Abrams, 2010. Ages 4–6.

One night in the library, Sam meets fellow mouse Sarah. Sam learns that Sarah is quite the explorer. She loves to scurry to the tops of shelves and explore the darkest corners of the building. Sam never climbs far up — he's too afraid! He prefers to research subjects — such as exploration — and write about them. Sarah doesn't know much about writing or research. Could reading and research help her learn more about the places she wishes to visit? Books in the library are grouped by subject. Show books about many different countries. Let children add the missing word to these verses and make up more verses.

My Aunt came back from old Japan
And brought to me
A frying _____ (pan).
My Aunt came back from ancient Rome.
And brought to me
A brush and _____ (comb).

Rosenthal, Betsy. *Which Shoes Would You Choose?* Illustrated by Nancy Cote. G.P. Putnam's Sons, 2010. Ages 2–4.

Sherman loves shoes! But which shoes are appropriate for his day? "Does Sherman wear skates when he goes out to eat? Of course not!

Dress shoes look great on his feet." Understanding which shoe should be worn for which occasion is an important lesson. After all, you can't wear your roller skates in the bathtub or your slippers to go mountain climbing! Ask each child to draw their favorite shoes and show where they would be worn.

Stringer, Lauren. *Winter Is the Warmest Season.* Harcourt, 2006. Ages 3–5.

Winter means warm coats, warm scarves, hot chocolate and hot breads, all of the warm things associated with cold weather. Ask: How might you group items for the other seasons of the year? For example, why might summer be the coldest season? Encourage children to name as many cold things as they can that are enjoyed in the summer.

Wilson, Karma. *The Cow Loves Cookies.* Illustrated by Marcellus Hall. McElderry Books, 2010. Ages 4–6.

As the farmer makes his rounds each day, most of the animals chew on the foods a young reader would expect. But when it's time to feed the cow, she feasts on a special treat. The horse loves hay, the chickens need feed, the geese munch on corn, the hogs devour slop, the dog eats treats, but THE COW LOVES COOKIES! Pin the name of one of the animals on each child's back. He does not know what it says so he asks yes or no questions of the other players until he can guess what animal he is.

Reversibility

The ability to understand that actions can move in reverse order usually does not occur until after the age of seven. Children after this age are increasingly able to hold parts of the story in their mind so they can process flashbacks or retell the tale from end to beginning.

Reversibility is integral to logic puzzles involving the ability to work a problem in both directions. It is essential to understand the order of events in time. A major understanding in mathematics is that the position of an object doesn't change the object and that the object can be reversed from one position to another and back again. Examples of reversibility are given below and are reprinted with permission of Dr. Robert Sweetland from www.homeofbob.com/pedagogy/theories/development/pre Op.html

1. Being able to move four objects from one position to another doesn't change the cardinality (the number of objects) as they can be reversed to the original position.

2. Being able to imagine water being poured from a measuring cup into a tall narrow container and then from the tall narrow container to a short wide container will have the same amount, because pouring it back into the tall container would reverse the process and the amount would still be the same.

3. Being able to take two wires of equal length, bend one, set them side by side and mentally reverse the process of unbending the wire to its original length and declaring them to be equal in length.

4. Knowing that if 3 + 4 = 7, then 7 - 4 = 3 is the reverse process. If you add four and get seven, then if you have seven and remove four the process has been reversed.

5. If exercise causes you to breathe faster, what could you do to breathe slower?

6. If water makes ice how can it be reversed?

7. Mixing paint and watching the color change. Can paint be made to go from light to dark to light again?

8. What about light from a flashlight? If we slowly add slips of waxed paper what happens? What if we remove them one at a time?

9. What about unrolling a ball of string? How long is it? If we roll it up and unroll it again how long will it be?

ACTIVITIES FOR REVERSIBILITY

A. Cut out panels from comic strips. Can the child put them in order from the end to the beginning?

B. Collect four books about different size animals. Ask the child the put the books in order beginning with the smallest animal and ending with the largest. Then ask the child to begin with the largest animal and end with the smallest.

C. Use black construction paper and white chalk. The child makes white dots showing (in order) where the main character was in the story. Example: Red Riding Hood was at home, in the forest and at Granny's cottage. Connect the dots with lines to create a story map.

Pictures of her home, trees for the forest and Granny's cottage can be drawn by the appropriate dots. Use the map to tell the story from the end to the beginning starting at granny's cottage.

D. Share the picture book *The Hat* by Jan Brett.

Cut apart the eight story strips that follow this paragraph. Read the strips aloud to the child/ren. Ask: Which happened last in the story? Which came next? Help the children to place the strips in order from the end to the beginning of the story (correct reverse order: 8, 1, 4, 3, 5, 6, 2, 7).

1. Animals take the clothes from the clothesline.
2. A sock falls to the ground.
3. Lisa finds Hedgie.
4. Lisa removes the sock from Hedgie's prickles.
5. The animals laugh at Hedgie's hat.
6. Hedgie gets the sock stuck on his prickles.
7. Lisa hangs her winter woolens on the line.
8. Lisa chases the animals.

E. Share a book about opposites, for example, *Exactly the Opposite* by Tana Hoban. Challenge children to complete the opposites listed below:

1. Cows are big but chicks are _____.
2. The barn is near but the moon is _____.
3. The sun shines during the _____.
4. Hedgie sees the moon at _____.
5. Stars are far away but house lights are _____.
6. The woods are big but the farmyard is _____.
7. Animals eat during the day but sleep at _____.
8. A mouse is little but a horse is _____.
9. Animals can be both big and _____.

BOOKS TO SHARE AND QUESTIONS TO ASK

Burton, Virginia Lee. *The Little House.* Houghton Mifflin, 1978. Ages 3–5.

The little house first stood in the country, but gradually the city grew closer and closer until the little house was surrounded by tall buildings. The only solution was to move the little house back to the country — a tale that ends where it begins. Create a map that shows the travels of the little house. Sing this song about *The Little House* to the tune of "Twinkle, Twinkle Little Star."

> *Sitting quiet as a mouse*
> *Was a very small pink (1)_____ [mouse].*
> *Saw the boys and girls have fun*
> *Playing in the morning (2)_____ [sun],*
> *Thought the countryside was pretty.*
> *Builders came and built a (3)_____ [city].*
> *At night couldn't see the moon*
> *Only saw the sun at (4)_____ [noon].*

Cannon, Janelle. *Stellaluna*. Scholastic, 1993. Ages 4–6.

Mother bat is flying one night when she meets an owl. In her attempts to escape the bird she drops her baby, Stellaluna. The young bat lands in a bird's nest where she is adopted by a mother bird. Stellaluna is fed insects (which she hates) and taught to sit on a branch right side up. "Following the house rules," says Mother Bird, "is very important." Stellaluna finally meets a family of bats and is recognized by her own mother. The bat family teaches Stellaluna bat ways, which include flying at night and eating sweet fruit as well as hanging upside down to sleep. When Stellaluna and the birds meet again they discover that they are both very alike and very different and that this does not keep them from being friends. Complete the bat information and sing to the tune of "London Bridge."

> *Little bats have _____ _____ (pointy*
> *ears) _____, _____.*
> *Little bats eat _____ and _____ (fruits*
> *and seeds)*
> *And _____ (fly at night).*

Fisher, Carolyn. *A Twisted Tale*. Knopf, 2002. Ages 3–5.

Bailey Tarbell is in a pickle. A tornado swooped down and sucked all the animals on her farm up into the air. When it finally spat them out again, they were all mixed up. The cow now clucks and tries to sit on eggs, the cat chases the dog, who hisses and runs up trees, the pig quacks, the duck moos, and the chickens are all rooting in the mud. Help Bailey sort the animals by the sounds. Sing to the tune of "Did You Ever See a Lassie?":

> *Did you ever see a chicken,*
> *A chicken, a chicken?*
> *Did you ever see a chicken,*
> *Eat corn on a farm?*

Gliori, Debi. *The Trouble with Dragons.* Walker, 2008. Ages 4–6.

The careless ways of dragons could cause the end of the Earth, unless they can find a way to turn things around. The world is populated by some beastly dragons who care nothing for how much they pollute the oceans, chop down the trees, gobble up all the food and use everything up without stopping to think. Those dragons need to wake up and do just the reverse of what they are doing to their world before it is too late. Ask: What are some things they could do to make a better world? Have children look at their hands. Name many positive things they can do with their hands to make a better world. Examples are clap, pat, and build.

Johnson, D.B. *Henry's Night.* Houghton Mifflin, 2009. Ages 5–7.

Henry cannot sleep. The sounds of the village keep him awake. If only he could find the whippoorwill, the night bird no one sees, and hear its sweet song! Henry takes his night jar, fills it with fireflies, and sets off with the lantern to track the elusive bird. But each time he draws near, the bird stops singing and flies deeper into the woods. Henry encounters many wonderful creatures there, but will he ever find his night bird? Ask: What creatures might he find if he walked in the day? Complete this pattern and sing to "Skip to My Lou." Henry saw:

> *Pokey turtles walking down the path,*
> *Fluffy bunnies hopping in the woods,*
>
> _____ _____ _____ _____ —
>
> *Look, little children, look!*

Kirsch, Vincent. *Natalie and Naughtily.* Bloomsbury, 2008. Ages 4–6.

Natalie and Naughtily Nopps live in a house on top of a big department store. Natalie loves visiting every floor from top to bottom! Naughtily? From bottom to top! One day the girls receive a note from their parents asking them NOT to play in the store that day! "Today we shall go to the store to help!" they agree. Evening gowns are on floor two, perfume and hats on three, coats on four — and on every floor there are customers galore. But will the girls really be any help? Or will they each be going in different directions?

Play: The Mystery Toy. Here are six clues about a toy that can be found in the toy department. Ask a child to name a number between one and six. Read the clue for that number. If the child passes, call on another child to give you a different number. The game continues until the mystery toy is guessed or all clues are read.

1. I can move.
2. I have more than one part to me.
3. I can make noise.
4. I am not an animal.
5. My name rhymes with rain.
6. I often go round and round. (Answer: Train).

LaRochelle, David. *The End*. Illustrated by Richard Eggielski. Scholastic, 2007. Ages 4–7.

"...And they lived happily ever after." So begins this wacky original fairy tale *The End*, which traces the courtship and marriage of a handsome knight and a beautiful princess — backwards! Before we reach the beginning, we meet a temperamental giant, a beleaguered cook, a dragon who's scared of bunny rabbits, an oversized tomato, and an impish figure on a flying pig who just might be the cause of all the madness. A tale to reread from the end to the beginning.

Sing to the tune of "If You're Happy and You Know It," and add more verses about other characters in the story.

If you change the R in ring to a K
If you change the R in ring to a K
If you change the R to K
Then a ring becomes a king
If you change the R in ring to a K.

If you change Dr in Dragon to a W
If you change Dr in Dragon to a W
If you change Dr to W
Then a dragon becomes a wagon
If you change Dr in Dragon to a W

Circle Stories by Laura Numeroff

Point out to children that the stories below by Laura Numeroff are "Circle Stories." Each story ends where it begins. If possible, draw or paste pictures of the items that each character asks for. Give out the pictures and challenge children to place the pictures in the order in which the items appear in the story.

Numeroff, Laura. *If You Give a Cat a Cupcake.* Illustrated by Felicia Bond. HarperCollins, 2008. Ages 3–5.

If you give a cat a cupcake, he'll ask for some sprinkles to go with it and he might spill some on the floor. Cleaning up will make him hot, so you'll give him a bathing suit — and that's just the beginning. A full circle tale that ends where it begins. Ask: If you took away one thing the cat needed how would the story change?

Numeroff, Laura. *If You Give a Pig a Party.* Illustrated by Felicia Bond. HarperCollins, 2005. Ages 3–5.

If you give a pig a party, she's going to ask for some balloons. Then she'll want to decorate the house. When she's finished, she'll put on her favorite dress. Then she'll call all her friends — Mouse, Moose, and more. Suppose Pig could not find her favorite dress. Ask: What might she wear?

Numeroff, Laura. *If You Take a Mouse to the Movies.* Illustrated by Felicia Bond. HarperCollins, 2000. Ages 3–5.

If you take a mouse to the movies, he'll ask you for some popcorn. When you give him the popcorn, he'll want to string it all together. Then he'll want to hang it on a Christmas tree and you'll have to buy him one. A full circle tale that ends where it begins. Suppose the movie house was closed that day. Ask: Where else could Mouse go?

Numeroff, Laura. *If You Take a Mouse to School.* Illustrated by Felicia Bond. HarperCollins, 2002. Ages 3–5.

If you take a mouse to school, he'll ask you for your lunch box. When you give him your lunch box, he'll want a sandwich to go in it. Then he'll need a notebook and some pencils. He'll probably want to share your backpack, too. A full circle tale that ends where it begins. Ask: What might you give Mouse at school so that he would keep busy and not keep asking for other things?

Polette, Keith. *Moon Over the Mountain*. Raven Tree Press, 2010. Ages 4–7.

A poor stonecutter wishes that he were a rich merchant, and the Spirit of the Desert grants his wish. When the stonecutter discovers that the sun has wilted his fruits and vegetables, he wishes that he were the sun. When the wind causes a dust storm and blots out the sun, he wishes to become the wind, and again his wish is granted. Next, he becomes a mountain. Agapito finally finds happiness when he wishes to become a coyote, because now his life is no longer set in stone. A tale that comes full circle. Ask: Why do you suppose the Spirit of the Desert kept granting Agapito wishes? Complete these patterns (an oral activity):

If I were the sun I could _____ and _____
But I couldn't _____ because the wind does that.
If I were the wind I could _____ and _____
But I couldn't _____ because the mountain does that.
If I were the mountain I could _____ and _____
But I couldn't _____ because coyote does that.

Singer, Marilyn. *Mirror, Mirror: A Book of Reversible Verse*. Dutton, 2010. Ages 5–8.

From *Snow White* to *The Ugly Duckling*, 14 familiar tales told in verse can be read from top to bottom or bottom to top. Only the capital letters and punctuation marks are changed. Ask: Is the story different when read from bottom to top? How?

Williams, Linda. *Horse in the Pigpen*. Illustrated by Megan Lloyd. HarperCollins, 2002. Ages 3–5.

What a reversible day! Something very strange is happening on this little farm. None of the animals are where they belong! Pigs are in the chicken coop and hens are in the dog house. The only person who can sort it all out is Ma — but Ma is terribly busy. What will the animals and one puzzled little girl do if Ma never has time to get everything back the way it's supposed to be? Make up sentences about the farm animals in which most words have the same beginning sound such as "pink pigs prefer pancakes." Complete the following:

Happy hens_____.

THREE

Building Word Power: Developing Verbal/Linguistic Thinking

Language Patterns

The young child's developing brain is a linguistic storehouse that holds not only words but also patterns of stories and poems and sentences and phrases. These patterns enter the memory through the ears and remain available for a lifetime of reading, writing, speaking, listening and thinking. The good reader is a person who looks at a page of print knowing that she will find clues that trigger the memory of familiar patterns. The reader is able to figure out much of the unknown because he recognizes the similarity between the new structures he is encountering and the structure or patterns he already knows.

A Variety of Language Experiences

1. Language patterns must be anchored in the brain before they can be recalled for speaking, reading and writing.

2. The majority of young children build this brain storehouse of language patterns by hearing the patterns repeated many times. Some researchers say a pattern must be heard at least 37 times before it becomes a part of the child's language storehouse.

3. The use of music and rhythm can speed up the process of building the language storehouse.

4. Poems and stories read aloud are essential tools for developing language skills and showing young children how language works.

5. Firsthand experiences, like a field trip, a puppet show, constructing models and play, all lead to the development of language skills.

6. Purely verbal experiences must be balanced with less verbal experiences, such as painting, dancing, pantomime, sculpting, music, rhythms, and play, which evoke thoughts and feelings that lead to the building of a strong language storehouse.

The Values of Reading Aloud to Young Children

Listening to the written word read aloud exposes children to language patterns they can internalize by hearing them again and again. It tunes children's ears to the pronunciation of words and to the cadences of various kinds of sentences in ways that print itself cannot. In sensing the love of the reader for the written word, children know why reading is important.

If you're wondering how to go about releasing children to rapid reading from the very start, try using this method, called echo reading:

When I'm happy
I'm happy.
When I'm sad
I'm sad.
When I smile
I smile.
When I'm bad
I'm bad.
When I swing
I swing.
Tree to tree
Tree to tree.

Can you guess
Can you guess,
I'm a chimpanzee!

Read the excerpt aloud several times, inviting the children to chime in as soon as they know how the poem is working. After they have it familiarly in mind, show them the print to read. They will chime it rapidly as they heard it, using only minimum clues to unlock a line of print or an entire couplet. An important value of this kind of chiming comes from children hearing themselves reading" with the poise and cadence of a mature reader. You can refer to their reading of "When I'm Happy" whenever you need a model of what good reading sounds like: "Let's read this page together the same way you read 'When I'm Happy.'"

Leader reads:	*Children echo:*
The other day	The other day
I met a bear	I met a bear
out in the woods	out in the woods
a way out there.	a way out there.

The other day I met a bear
out in the woods a way out there.

He looked at me.	He looked at me.
I said "good day."	I said "good day."
I looked at him.	I looked at him.
He ran away.	He ran away.

He looked at me. I said "good day."
I looked at him. He ran away.

Bill Martin, Jr., the author of the beloved *Brown Bear, Brown Bear*, wrote books for young children based on the premise that every child is already something of an expert in analyzing language, a fact overlooked in most reading programs. The activities in this chapter are based on this premise. Think of the young child on a bus who says, "I ringed the bell," a sentence he never in his life heard, yet he gives evidence that he is analyzing language and that he knows how to change a verb from present to past tense. In similar ways the reading program must help children become aware of what they intuitively know about language and must help them explore and verbalize the relationship between their old and new learnings.

ACTIVITIES TO DEVELOP
VERBAL/LINGUISTIC SKILLS

One activity to help develop verbal/linguistic skills is the lively experimenting with the various sentence patterns. Two sentence patterns that have proved especially useful for this kind of experimentation are (1) vocabulary substitution, and (2) expanding a sentence.

The first of the activities is to use the exact structure of a sentence as the basis for creating a semantically new sentence. Your first step in helping children learn this skill is to choose a model sentence and copy it on the chalkboard, leaving space between each word.

After sharing a book about cows or farm animals, your conversation goes something like this:

> Children, I'm going to draw a line to the word cow. Now, supposing we didn't want to use the word cow, what other words could we use instead of cow?

Suggestions will begin to flow.

I never saw a purple cow.

horse

pig

rabbit

> Children, all of our naming words are animals. Suppose we wanted another kind of naming word — one that would make a spooky sentence.

I never saw a purple cow.

horse

pig

rabbit

spook

vampire

Now, children, suppose we didn't want to use the word purple. Who else has a describing word?

Again the suggestions will flow.

I never saw a purple cow.

brown horse

pink pig

> hungry rabbit
> silly spook
> green vampire

Children, does anyone in this class like silly sentences? Well, I'm going to give you a new action word that will really make a silly sentence.

I never saw	a purple cow.
kissed	a brown horse
petted	a pink pig
cooked	a hungry rabbit
married	a silly spook
tickled	a green vampire

And so it goes until the children have suggested vocabulary substitutions for all of the words. You may wish to enter the game, especially if the children are not having fun with the substitutions they suggest. Now the lid is off and the children's merriment knows no bounds as they contemplate other combinations like kissing purple vampires and marrying pink spooks.

Expanding Sentences

Expanding sentences is another technique for helping children become aware of the shape of sentences and for helping them develop this awareness into reading and writing and speaking skills. This sentence manipulation is exactly what the term *expanding* connotes. Any simple sentence can be expanded by adding phrases, clauses or words.

Share any fairy tale and use the main character in the following sentence expansion activity:

Children, let's make this sentence longer.

This is the story of Cinderella.

Let's see if we can think of some describing words to put in front of "Cinderella."

This   is   the   story   of   Cinderella.
> funny
> kind
> nice

Now let's think of some describing words to put in front of "story."

This is the story of Cinderella.
rhyming   funny
silly   kind
impossible nice

Now who would like to try reading a sentence using any of the words on the board? Have you noticed, boys and girls, how our sentence is getting longer and longer?

There is one other way we can expand this sentence and make it even longer. We can add a whole collection of words that belong together.

This is the story of Cinderella
rhyming   funny   who lost her teeth
silly   kind   who likes to bake cakes
impossible nice   who stands on her head.

An expanded sentence can be more dramatic, "paint more pictures," or produce a more interesting array of sounds, but *it is not necessarily a better sentence.* However, in the process of expanding sentences, children become keenly aware of the placement and function of phrases and clauses and individual words within a sentence. This in itself is a valuable reading skill. It is the skill of anticipating how a sentence is working.

Building Word Power

Let children dictate word lists that arise from a story you have shared. Thirteen words are needed to create a chant. For example, you could share *Horton Hatches the Egg* by Dr. Seuss:

Horton, the elephant volunteers to sit on Mayzie's egg to give her a rest. When she doesn't return, Horton is captured by hunters and sold to a circus where people pay one cent to see an elephant sitting on an egg.

Here are things found in a circus:

Circus Things

_____ clowns

_____ elephants

_____ lions

_____ tigers

_____ horses

_____ acrobats

Put a describing word in front of each.		*Put an action word in front of each.*	
Funny	clowns	Jumping	clowns
Fat	elephants	Dancing	elephants
Tawny	lions	Roaring	lions
Striped	tigers	Leaping	tigers
White	horses	Prancing	horses
Colorful	acrobats	Swinging	acrobats

These are just few.

In the second verse, tell where you would see them.

clowns	in a car
elephants	in the ring
lions	on a stand
tigers	in a cage
horses	in a parade
acrobats	in the air

Popcorn venders, too.

Stand and shout!

Bring them out!

Circus things!

Reading and Writing Strategies for Any Picture Book

1. **Topic Talking:** Assign partners. Partner A speaks to Partner B on a topic related to the story for a short period of time until the teacher says "switch." Then Partner B speaks to Partner A on the same topic until the teacher says "stop." The procedure is repeated for a second and third round increasing the talking time each round.

2. **Find Someone Who:** Read aloud six to eight statements related in general to the story to be shared. Example: For *Hansel and Gretel* find someone who has walked in the woods, who has made a gingerbread house, who can name a story with a witch? Children who can do or have done each of the statements raise their hands.

3. **Topic Focusing:** From *Annie and the Wild Animals*, guess yes or no: (A) Black bears are clowns of the woods, (B) Black bears can be both black and brown. Support or deny guesses by listening to this poem about black bears:

> Climbing up or climbing down
> The black bear is a funny clown.
> He's sometimes black and sometimes brown.

The idea here is to get children curious about a topic. Whatever the book is about, ask questions on the topic that can be answered with numbers or yes or no. Then share the answers before reading the story.

4. **Rank Order:** Share any picture book about food (two are *Cloudy with a Chance of Meatballs* and *The Wolf's Chicken Stew*). Take turns. Cut out pictures of foods from magazines. Choose four. Put the pictures in order from the most to the least favorite.

5. **Sharing:** Use any picture story book that demonstrates the concept of sharing. Example: *The Little Old Woman and the Hungry Cat* by Nancy Polette.

6. **Responding in Song:** Complete this song about the above story (tune: "Are You Sleeping?").

_____ *cat* _____ *cat*
_____ *(where?)* _____ *(where?)*
_____ *and* _____ *(doing what?)*
_____ *and* _____ *(doing what?)*

Read this book. Read this book.

Word choices will vary:

Hungry cat, Greedy cat—
In the house, On the road—
Eating and walking, talking and sewing.

7. **Pre Reading Skills:** Look at the title: *The Little Old Woman and the Hungry Cat.* (Adapt this exercise to fit any title that is shared.)

    A. Clap the number of syllables for each word in the title.
    B. Find the two longest words.
    C. Find a word that rhymes with hat.
    D. Find a word where the *O* says its name.
    E. Have children stand. Spell each word in the title. If a letter goes above the line, children stretch arms above their heads; if below the line, children touch their knees with both hands; if on the line children stretch arms straight out.

BOOKS AND ACTIVITIES FOR VERBAL/LINGUISTIC SKILLS

ABC Books

Ashman, Linda. *M Is for Mischief.* Illustrated by Nancy Carpenter. Dutton, 2008. Ages 5–7.

An A–Z book describing 26 naughty children by the use of alliteration: "Offensive Oscar refuses to wash." Each child finds that bad behavior has its unhappy consequences. Name positive feelings that begin with different letters of the alphabet. As children think of words the leader constructs the words with magnetic letters on a metal cookie sheet.

Burningham, John. *John Burningham's ABC.* Crown, 2000. Ages 2–4.

Simple identification of pictures, one for each letter. Activity: small groups search old magazines to cut out items for each letter of the alphabet and paste them in order on large sheets of paper.

Geisert, Arthus. *Country Road ABC.* Houghton Mifflin, 2010. Ages 4–6.

An illustrated journey through America's farmland takes readers along a country road past farms, small towns, and churches. Many country items introduced with each letter of the alphabet (*E* is for erosion) will be unfamiliar to young children but are explained in a glossary. Put the poem in ABC order by the girls' names. Read about jobs done on a farm.

1. Flora milked the cow
2. Betty chased a rat
3. Dina found a cat
4. Alice picked tomatoes
5. Emma hoed the garden
6. Hannah fed the sow
7. Carla wore blue jeans
8. Gina rode a frisky horse

Grossman, Bill. *My Little Sister Hugged an Ape.* Illustrated by Kevin Hawkes. Knopf, 2004. Ages 4–6.

Many animals are presented in rollicking verse and bold illustrations. Little Sister will show how much she likes wild animals by hugging them all, from Ape to Zebra, whether they like it or not! A newt, an octopus, a porcupine — it's a slimy, slippery, prickly situation. What will Little Sister hug next? And what kind of trouble will those hugs get her into? Gather as many books about different wild animals as possible. Let children arrange them in ABC order using the first letter of each animal name.

Mora, Pat. *Marimba! Marimba! Animals from A–Z.* Illustrated by Doug Cushman. Clarion, 2006. Ages 3–6.

After the visitors have left the zoo and the animals have settled down for the night, a mischievous monkey starts a ting-tong rhythm on the marimba and slowly the animals awaken. Lions and llamas samba and cougars and coyotes conga as all the animals join in the fun to create a rollicking fiesta. Let the children practice several ways of saying hello (*bonjour, buenos dias*, etc.). If a child has relatives from another country ask the child to learn how to say "hello" in that language and teach it to the class.

Schnur, Steven, *Summer, An Alphabet Acrostic*. Clarion, 2001. Ages 3–6.

Acrostic poems from A to Z describe summer. *A* is for awnings and each letter in the word describes summer awnings. *B* is for beach and the word beach is described in an acrostic. This is an excellent pattern for writing about the other seasons. Give children these separate cut out letters: P, S, R, N, G, I.

Use three letters to make a word that rhymes with win. Let's use pin as an example.

> Take away the P and add two letters to make a word that means smile (grin).
>
> Take away two letters and add a beginning letter and an ending letter to tell what you can do to music (sing).
>
> Use all of the letters to make a word that is a season of the year (spring).

Shannon, George. *Tomorrow's Alphabet*. Illustrated by Donald Crews. Greenwillow, 1996.

Do you know the alphabet well enough to play with it? If so, this is the book for you! In tomorrow's alphabet you have to think ahead:

> A is for seed, tomorrow's apple.
>
> B is for egg, tomorrow's bird.
>
> Q is for scraps, tomorrow's quilt.
>
> The *Q* is a pattern about change. *Scraps* are only *scraps* until *they are sewn together* and then they become a *quilt*.
>
> Try this one: Snowflakes are only snowflakes until _____ and then they become _____.

Sobel, June. *Shiver Me Letters: A Pirate ABC*. Illustrated by Henry Cole. Harcourt, 2006. Ages 4–6.

The captain of this brave and bumbling pirate crew has ordered them to capture the entire alphabet — and they'll walk the plank if they're missing a single letter! Now these swashbuckling mateys are embarking on an alphabet adventure unlike any other, and they won't (ahem, can't) rest until they've found an A, a Z, and everything in between. Choose one letter of the alphabet and draw as many things as you can that begin with that letter.

Sweet, Melissa. *Carmine: A Little More Red.* Houghton Mifflin, 2005. Ages 6–8.

An ABC book that tells an updated Red Riding Hood story of a little girl going to granny's for alphabet soup. The little girl is a painter, always in search of just the right color (especially anything in the red family) to add to her paintings. So she is too easily lured by a lovely meadow full of poppies. And, as she begins painting, she is oblivious to danger lurking along the path. Ask: How many ways is this story like *Little Red Riding Hood?* How is it different? Ask children to name colors they see around the room. Each child is to choose one color and make up a sentence about themselves using that color. (Avoid "I like [color].")

Poetry

Esbaum, Jill. *Stanza.* Illustrated by Jack E. Davis. Harcourt, 2009. Ages 4–6.

Stanza is a bully who eats chicken pot pie and writes poetry, hoping that his brothers never find out. But what if he wins the poetry contest? Along the way he learns that writing poetry takes lots of effort. Ask children to give different rhyming words to end this two-line poem: This cereal will not make you fat, so feed it to a skinny _____.

Krensky, Stephen. *There Once Was a Very Odd School.* Illustrated by Tamara Petrosino. Dutton, 2004. Ages 4–8.

A great introduction to limericks. These poke fun at the many facets of school life. Just in time for back-to-school book bags, here is a collection of limericks about a very unusual school. From the super-jock who is so shy he can barely say hello to the weird teacher whose students are mysteriously turning into statues, readers will laugh themselves silly at all the fun that makes up one very odd school year.

Ask children to add the missing words to these lines:

A donkey went to my school to see what he could see.
What do you think he saw? _____

A donkey went to my school to take what he could take.
What do you think he took? _____
A donkey went to my school to get what he could get.
What do you think he got? _____

Raczka, Bob. *Guyku*. Illustrated by Peter Reynolds. Houghton Mifflin, 2010. Ages 7–10.

A year of haiku for boys. "Last week's snowman looks/under the weather. Must be/a spring allergy." When you're a guy, nature is one big playground — no matter what the season. There are puddles to splash in during spring, pine trees to climb in summer, maple seeds to catch in fall, and icicles to swordfight with in winter. So what kind of poetry best captures these special moments, at a length that lets guys get right back to tree-climbing and kite-flying? Why, guyku, of course! Challenge older students to write a haiku using the 5-7-5 syllable pattern.

Wardlaw, Lee. *Won Ton: A Cat Tale Told in Haiku*. Illustrated by Eugene Yelchin. Henry Holt, 2011. Ages 6–9.

This tale of a shelter cat and a boy who takes him home is told in haiku

Nice place they got here
Bed. Bowl. Blankie. Just like home
Or so I've been told.

Older students might enjoy trying to write haiku using the 5-7-5 syllable pattern.

Words! Words! Words!

Banks, Kate. *Max's Words*. Illustrated by Boris Kulikov. Farrar, 2006. Ages 5–7,

When his classmates bring their collections to school, Max has nothing to collect until he discovers words! So Max decides to start a collection of his own. He's going to collect words. He starts with small words that he cuts out of newspapers and magazines, but soon his collection has spilled out into the hallway. Benjamin brags that he has one thousand stamps. But a thousand stamps is really just a bunch of stamps. A pile of words, however, can make a story. Ask children to name some (1) name words, (2) describing words, (3) action words that end in "ed." Take a word from each group to make simple sentences (example: Pink pig jumped).

Beard, Alex. *The Jungle Grapevine*. Abrams, 2010. Ages 4–6.

When bird mixes up something turtle says, bird accidentally starts a rumor about the watering hole drying up. One rumor leads to another and soon the jungle animals are in an uproar. Can peace ever be restored to the animal kingdom? Play the telephone game, with one child whispering a message which is passed from child to child. Ask: Is the message at the end of the game the same as at the beginning?

Birdseye, Tom. *Look Out Jack! The Giant Is Back!* Illustrated by Will Hillenbrand. Holiday House, 2001. Ages 4–7.

The brother of the giant that Jack killed is angry and after Jack's hide. He follows Jack to America with feet so stinky that geese faint in midair. Readers will enjoy the tall tale exaggerations and be inspired to try some of their own. Explain what exaggeration is and point out examples from the story. Ask children to finish these sentences using exaggeration:

It was SO hot that _____.
It was SO cold that _____.
The wind blew SO hard that _____.
The rain was SO heavy that _____.

Bright, Paul. *Quiet!* Illustrated by Guy Parker-Rees. Orchard Books, 2003. Ages 3–6.

Mama Lion was upset that baby Leo couldn't take his nap — the jungle was too noisy! When Papa Lion yelled "quiet" there was not a rumble nor a grumble, not a chitter nor a chatter, not a pitter nor a patter, not a teeny, tiny squeak. Now Papa Lion must make sure it stays this way as baby Leo sleeps. It got as quiet as_____. Ask students to complete these similes:

It was as light as a _____.
As cold as _____.
As green as _____.
As hard as a _____.
As soft as _____.

As strong as _____.
As deep as the _____.
As dark as _____.
As hungry as _____.
As sweet as _____.

Capucilli, Alyssa Satin. *Inside a Zoo in the City*. Illustrated by Ted Arnold. Scholastic, 2000. Ages 3–6.

A fun cumulative rebus tale introducing zoo animals. A squawking parrot wakes a stalking tiger and disturbs the sleep of a lion that roars. A symphony of chattering and barking ensues, as all the animals race from the dormitory where they live to the zoo in time to greet the visitors. Encourage children to create their own rebus stories, substituting pictures cut from old magazines for words.

Dunrea, Olivier. *Gossie*. Houghton Mifflin, 2011. Ages 2–4.

A bilingual board book about a small yellow gosling that likes to wear bright red boots. Every day. Until the day her boots disappear. She looks everywhere for them: under the bed, over the wall, even in the barn. Preschoolers will enjoy searching for the boots. Let children act out this foot poem:

This is my right foot.
I'll raise it up high (Raise and lower right foot).
This is my left foot,
Touching the sky (raise and lower left foot).
Can't find my boot (put hand over eyes and look around),
So I'll put on my shoe (mime putting on shoe)—
First right, then left.
Now I'm wearing two!

Fleming, Denise. *Shout! Shout It Out!* Henry Holt, 2011. Ages 2–4.

By taking basic learning concepts like numbers, letters and colors and putting them on display the author asks kids to shout out what they know making learning a game. Let children sing familiar Mother Goose rhymes either to music they know or music they make up. After each rhyme is read, ask: Could this really happen? Why or why not? Example: Yes, Mary could probably take a lamb to school and Boy Blue could sleep under a haystack, but could anyone grow a garden with silver bells or would the king's soldiers put together a smashed egg?

Frank, John. *The Toughest Cowboy or How the Wild West Was Tamed.* Illustrated by Zachary Pullen. Simon & Schuster, 2004. Ages 5–7.

How do you tame the roughest cowpoke ever to ride the open range? He uses barbed wire for dental floss and drinks 32 ounces of hot Tabasco sauce every day. The only way to tame this cowboy is with a little dog, of course! So he sets off to town to find one. Great examples of exaggeration. Challenge children to orally complete these phrases using exaggeration:

The cowboy was so tall that _____.

His voice was so loud that_____.

Gorbachev, Valeri. *Dragon Is Coming!* Harcourt, 2009. Ages 4–6.

Little Mouse misunderstands the words he hears and warns all the animals that the rumbling they hear is an approaching dragon. Mouse is certain that a big gray dragon flying overhead will spell doom for her and her animal friends. So she makes it her mission to lead everyone to the safety of the barn. But it seems as though nothing will stop this hideous creature. Then the barn doors squeak open slowly — revealing what everyone has been dreading. Let the children guess what is behind the door. Clues: Guess the name of each storybook character with the help of the clues (given one at a time):

1. Hungry dog, bone, bare cupboard (Old other Hubbard).
2. Seven friends, wicked queen, princess (Snow White).
3. Hot porridge, broken chair, little girl, three bears).

Encourage children to give clues for their favorite stories.

Jansson, Tove. *Moomin's Little Book of Words.* Farrar, 2010. Ages 2–4.

Moomintroll takes the youngest reader through a day in his life, building simple vocabulary along the way. Point to each item. Say the word. Let the child point to the same item and repeat the word.

Lester, Helen. *Batter Up Wombat.* Illustrated by Lynn Munsinger. Houghton Mifflin, 2006. Ages 5–7.

This is a brand-new baseball season, and the Champs are ready to go in their spiffy clean uniforms. But when a wombat wanders onto the field on opening-game day, the Champs have no idea just how different the game is about to become. To Wombat, home plate is a dish, a bat is a furry creature, a pitcher is a container for milk and a foul is a chicken. When he is told to steal third base, he doesn't know where to hide it.

Sing the Story

Directions: Choose words from the box to complete each line in the song (tune: "Hush Little Baby"):

> fans   play   foul   base   word

A wombat wandered by one day.
A baseball team asked him to (1) _____.
Lots of rules the wombat heard,
Double meanings every (2) _____.
Hit the ball, began to race,
Picked it up and stole third (3) _____.
Then the fans began to howl.
The umpire said the ball was (4) _____.
A big black cloud came near the stands.
He dug a tunnel, saved the (5) _____.

Martin, Bill, Jr. *Baby Bear, Baby Bear What Do You See?* and *Panda Bear, Panda Bear, What Do You See?* Illustrated by Eric Carle. Henry Holt, 2011. Ages 2–4.

Classic preschool books to introduce pre-reading concepts of rhyme, rhythm and repetition. Encourage children to join in as they see the pictures and listen to the rhyming text.

McCall, Francis. *A Huge Hog Is a Big Pig.* Illustrated by Patricia Keeler. Greenwillow, 2002. Ages 6–8.

Ever play a wacky word game sometimes called Stinky Pinky or Silly Willy? First you get a two-word clue. Then you think of two words that mean the same thing and rhyme. A chubby kitty is a fat cat. Figure out the answers, then make up your own clues and answers. Examples below:

A light brown SUV is a _____(tan van).

A hen who doesn't feel well is a _____(sick chick).

Rosenthal, Amy. *Cookies.* Illustrated by Jane Dyer. HarperCollins, 2006. Ages 4–6.

Words are defined using cookies. Example: Polite — "Thank you very much for sharing your cookies with me." Ask the child/ren to pretend they have a cookie or use real cookies. Give a word: proud, modest, respect, fair, unfair, pessimistic, optimistic, polite, envy, loyal, open-minded, trustworthy, regret. Ask for oral examples of the meaning of the word using their cookie. Other children will guess the word being demonstrated. Example: I have never tasted these cookies but I am sure they will be good. (Optimistic)

Sacre, Antonio. *A Mango in the Hand.* Illustrated by Sebastia Serra. Abrams, 2011. Ages 4–6.

When Fransisco has trouble gathering mangos his father tells him, "Where there's a will, there's a way." When Fransisco gets home after sharing the mangos with his grandmother and aunt he tells his father, "Sometimes it's better to give than to receive." Here is a tale told in proverbs. Explain what a proverb is and give the children half of a proverb. Ask: How would you finish it?

Don't cry over (spilt milk).

You can lead a horse to water but (you can't make him drink it).

When the cat's away (the mice will play).

Shannon, George. *White Is for Blueberry.* Illustrated by Laura Dronzek. Greenwillow, 2005. Ages 3–5.

Is a blueberry blue? Is a crow black? Is fire yellow? Is snow white? If you think you know, then think — and look again! "White is for blueberry when still too young to pick." A book about objects that change color depending on when we look, how near and how far. Let the children choose one object from the book that changes color and illustrate the object in its two different colors. Ask children to identify other items in nature represented by each color: green, red, orange, yellow, brown.

Stringer, Lauren. *Winter Is the Warmest Season.* Harcourt, 2006. Ages 3–5.

Winter is warm coats, warm scarves, hot chocolate and hot breads, all of the warm things associated with cold weather. How many more can children name? Create a season chant. Thirteen items are needed, six in the first verse and seven in the second.

SUMMER THINGS

Ice cream	Soft breeze
Sun screen	Air conditioning
Bathing suit	Baseball
Brisk fan	Picnics
Swimming pool	Growing gardens
Popsicles —	Wildflowers
	Sunny days, too.

These are just a few.

From near and far
Here they are
SUMMER THINGS!

Walton, Rick. *That's My Dog.* G.P. Putnam's Sons, 2001. Ages 4–6.
What could be better than having a dog?
Having a big dog!
And what could be better than having a big dog?
Having a big, bouncy, slobbery dog!

Meet one proud little dog owner as he conjures up one great dog. Sentence expansion beginning with "A big red dog" and adding a word at a time to achieve: "He's my big, red, happy, muddy, smart, bouncy, slobbery, sneaky, stinky dog!" Children will have fun expanding other sentences. Example:

The _____ monkey sits in the

_____ tree.

The _____ cat sits on the _____ fence.

FOUR

Developing the Creative Mind

Creative Thinking: A Whole-Brain Process

Creative thinking is a whole-brain process. Whether it results in new methods, procedures or products, every area of the brain is used. The upper right quadrant visualizes, creates and intuits. The lower right quadrant inspires and motivates. The lower left quadrant organizes and the upper left critiques. All are essential elements in the creative process. Eleanor Duckworth states in her book *Piaget Rediscovered* that "the goal of education is to create men who are capable of doing new things, not simply repeating what other men have done — men who are creative, inventive discoverers."

The creative process requires one to become sensitive to problems or gaps in knowledge, to formulate and test solutions and to communicate results to others. If this seems beyond the capability of the preschool or primary child, think again! In Arnold Lobel's *Frog and Toad Together*, these two friends must work together to become aware of and solve many problems. In the story "Cookies," they decide that if they continue to eat the cookies they will get sick. They then *identify the difficulties in* not eating the cookies which are readily available. They *search for solutions*. First, they try putting the cookies in a box but discover they can easily open the box. They then try other solutions. They put a string around the box. They put the box on a high shelf. Nothing works. Finally, they *hypothesize* that the birds might like the cookies, so to *test the hypothesis* they take the box outside and call for the birds. Sure enough, "Birds

63

come from everywhere. They picked up all the cookies in their beaks and flew away." The *problem was solved.* "Now we have no more cookies to eat," said Toad sadly as he *communicates* the results to Frog.

What Are the Creative Thinking Skills?

There are four types of productive thinking that can lead to the development of the creative mind:

FLUENCY

Fluency is the process of brainstorming or coming up with many responses. The goal is quantity rather than quality, so no response is rejected. Questions to foster fluent thinking include those that follow:

How many things can we name that are wiggly, silly, quiet, prickly, hot, odd, tiny, large, long, smelly, heavy, high? Share *Things That Are Most* by Judi Barrett.

Use any picture for a good starter for a fluency activity and ask:

How many words can we give to describe this picture?

How many action sentences can we say about this picture?

How many reasons can we give for having a dinosaur as a pet?

Connect fluency questions to literature:

Cinderella must cook all the meals. The stepsisters like desserts. Ask the children to suggest as many desserts as they can for Cinderella to make.

Keeping the house spic and span is a job that requires many tasks. Ask the children to list all of the tasks they can think of that are necessary for Cinderella to do each day.

FLEXIBILITY

Flexibility requires responding in a variety of categories and/or finding new uses for familiar objects. Finding new categories stretches the mind beyond the expected response. These are a few sample questions:

1. Group the desserts listed in the fluency section by the seasons or months of the year in which they would most likely be made. In what other ways might the desserts be grouped?

2. A broom is normally used to sweep up crumbs, trash or dirt. How many other uses can you think of for a broom?

3. *B* is for Giant. Why? Give many answers. *A* is for zoo. Why? Share *Q Is for Duck* by Mary Elting.

4. How many uses can you think of for a twelve-inch stick? For a spoon?

5. How many ways can you group items found in a kitchen? Label each group.

6. Before sharing *Horton Hatches the Egg* by Dr. Seuss ask different children to choose one sentence starter such as those below to complete orally. Stress that there is no one right way to complete a sentence. Can each child come up with more than one way to complete the sentence they choose?

    A. Going to a circus would be _____.
    B. Keeping a promise is important because _____.
    C. When winter comes the animals in the woods _____
    _____.
    D. To be lazy means _____.
    E. When a bird lays an egg _____.
    F. Places to see an elephant are _____.
    G. If I had an elephant for a pet I would _____.
    H. I know it is spring when _____.

ORIGINALITY

Responding in new ways and creating new products or new solutions to problems encourages originality. Asking questions similar to the examples help a child develop their own originality:

1. Suppose the Fairy Godmother had not appeared to help Cinderella. How many other ways might Cinderella have arrived at the ball?

2. How might Cinderella create a beautiful ball gown from things she would find around the house?

3. Can you think of original solutions to these problems?

A. How can the prince get through a forest of thorns (without getting hurt) to rescue Sleeping Beauty?

B. How can Little Boy Blue keep from going to sleep?

C. How can Bo Peep find her lost sheep?

D. How many ways can Humpty Dumpty be put back together again?

4. Choose any two words and complete this sentence: A/n _____ is like a/n _____ because _____. Do not choose two living things to compare; however you can choose one living and one non living thing if you wish.

Here is an example: An alligator is like a store because it is always seeking new food to fill its dark cupboards.

alligator	melon	desert	basket	feather	pen
garden	monkey	laugh	fork	wrench	sail
zipper	bubble	soap	store	ocean	waterfall
net	hiccup	spring	pain	star	baseball
book	jet	shoe	ruler	canoe	computer
tree	insect	reptile	fish	parent	sibling
train	disease	shrub	rock	tent	lightning
horse	food	dessert	car	square	monster
field	sandal	sand	rooster	valley	vegetable
rain	cave	piano	guitar	well	sunshine
river	salad	wagon	stew	cliff	football

5. Share any picture book about one or more seasons.

To celebrate winter, ask the children to move as if they were:

Making snow angels.

Building a snowman.

A bird searching for seeds under the snow.

A goose flying south to escape the cold.

Ask what movements children can suggest for other seasons.

ELABORATION

Elaboration means adding to a product to enhance it or make it more complete. Sample questions follow:

1. In the Cinderella tale she lost her slipper. What could she add to the slipper so that it would be hard to lose?

2. Amelia Bedelia wears a maid's uniform. What could she add to her uniform to make it a dress every woman would want?

3. How many ways can you make a sandwich without bread?

4. One of the three pigs built a house of straw. What could he add to the house to make it so strong the wolf could not blow it down?

5. The animals all made fun of frog's swimsuit. What could frog add to the suit so that every one of the animals would want one like it?

6. Encourage children to elaborate on the stories that are read to them. Ask where could they add sound words and if there is an appropriate place to add a chant or two rhyming lines. For example, after each little pig builds his house the children might chant:

Look at my house, it's done, done, done.

I'll invite my friends and have fun, fun, fun!

7. Ask what they could add to this cookie jar to keep a thief from stealing the cookies.

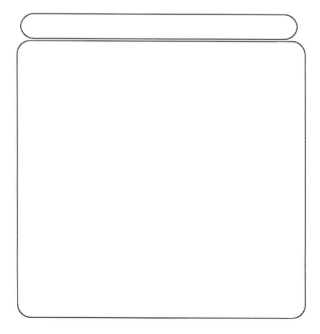

Books to Stimulate Creative Thinking

Baker, Keith. *Just How Long Can a String Be?* Scholastic, 2009. Ages 4–6.

> How many uses can you name for a ball of string? Use a string to measure. Have the children guess, in inches:
>
> How long is the desk? _____
> This jar is how many inches around? _____
> How tall is this chair? _____
> What other guesses can we make?
>
> Unwind a ball of string to measure each item and use a ruler or yardstick to measure the string and confirm or deny guesses.

Barretta, Gene. *Zoola Palooza*. A Christy Ottaviano Book, 2011. Ages 5–8.

> The all-animal touring concert group Zoola Palooza has come to town. With a motley crew of animals playing a variety of instruments, homographs (words spelled the same but with different meanings) abound. Billy the striped bass opens the show wearing a big bow tie. He gives a gracious bow from the top of his bass fiddle. Challenge children to make up sentences using these homographs:
>
> bat (a club) bat (an animal), ball (a round object) ball (a formal dance), bark (tree covering) bark (sound a dog makes), bowl (a dish) bowl (a game), date(month/year) date (food), gum (that holds teeth) gum (that you chew).

Bauer, Marion Dane. *If You Had a Nose Like an Elephant's Trunk.* Illustrated by Susan Winter. Holiday House, 2001. Ages 3–5.

> A great introduction to creative play. Ask: What would you do if you had cheeks like a chipmunk or a tail like a monkey? Suppose you woke up one morning with a giraffe's neck, an elephant's trunk, rabbit ears, or zebra stripes. Choose one and tell the story:
>
> One morning I woke up with _____. When people saw me, they _____. One problem that the _____ caused was _____. One good thing about having _____ was _____. I went to the _____ for help in getting rid of the _____, but he/she/they could

not help. The next morning when I woke up, the _____ was/were gone but instead I had _____.

Biel, Karen. *Jack's House.* Illustrated by Mike Wohnoutka. Holiday House, 2008. Ages 3–5.

Brainstorm all of the workers and tools needed to build a house then share this tale with a new twist that introduces many house-building machines and complete this pattern abut a hammer:

WHAT I'D LIKE TO BE WRITING PATTERN

I wish I were	I wish I were
A construction worker	A hammer
Building tall buildings	(Doing what?) _____
Sitting high in my steam shovel	(Doing what?) _____
Smiling.	Pounding.

Bond, Felicia. *The Day It Rained Hearts.* Harper-Collins, 2002. Ages 4–6.

The day it rained hearts Cornelia Augusta used them to create surprising valentines for her most unusual friends. Excellent example of originality. Ask: What unusual items could you use to create a valentine? Make a newspaper valentine. Cut out a heart. Put a friend's name on the heart. Staple a 12-inch ribbon to the heart. Paste or staple to the ribbon big words cut from the newspaper that say nice things about your friend. Examples: Great! Special! Wonderful! Super!

Brown, Margaret Wise. *The Golden Egg Book.* Illustrated by Leonard Weisgard. Random House reissue, 2004. Ages 3–5.

Guess what's inside the egg that bunny finds. Bunny handles the egg very carefully and finds a new friend after his nap. Do echo reading of the Egg Chant with children repeating each line after the leader:

AN EGG CHANT
We like eggs.
Big eggs
Small eggs
Oval eggs
White eggs
Brown eggs

Scrambled eggs.
These are just a few.

We like eggs.
In a basket
On the ground
In a nest
On a plate
In a pan
In the grass
On a shelf, too.

Stand and shout!
Bring them out!

We like eggs!

Carlson, Nancy. *Henry's Amazing Imagination.* Puffin Books, 2008. Ages 4–6.

At Show and Tell Time Henry shares amazing adventures and everyone thinks he is a fibber. How can Henry stop the truth from getting mixed up with his imagination? Read aloud this verse from "Sing Taddle O'Day" (Anonymous):

Once I had a little dog,
The color it was brown.
I teached him how to whistle,
To sing and dance and run.
His legs they were fourteen yards long,
His ears so very wide.
Around the world in half a day
On him I could ride.

Ask the children: "Could any parts of this verse not be true? Why?"

Conahan, Carolyn. *The Big Wish.* Chronicle Books, 2010. Ages 4–6.

What would be the biggest thing one could possibly wish for? Molly knows that she will have a chance to make the biggest wish ever. Ask the children to name an animal or an object. Tell what its biggest wish would be. For example, a sail might wish to cross the finish line first. A star might wish to have only beautiful wishes wished upon it.

Connor, Leslie. *Miss Bridie Chose a Shovel.* Illustrated by Mary Azarian. Houghton Mifflin, 2004. Ages 4–6.

A young immigrant chooses a shovel to take with her on her travels and finds many uses for it. Ask: How many can you name?

In the winter out you go
> To shovel falling_____(snow).
> Put on your oldest shirt
> To shovel garden _____(dirt).
> For hungry hens you'll need
> To shovel chicken _____(feed).

Dodds, Dayle Ann. *Henry's Amazing Machine.* Illustrated by Kyrsten Brooker. Farrar, Straus & Giroux, 2004. Ages 5–7.

Ask: How many uses can you think of for Henry's machine? It is getting larger and larger and what it does is a surprise for everyone.

A BIG MACHINE RAP

Divide into three groups. Group one chants the first verse three times. After group one chants the verse once, group two begins to chant verse two and chants it two times. After group two chants its verse one time, group three chants its verse. All should end at the same time.

> (1) Chug, chug. chug a lug
> Dig a hole, find a bug.
> Chug, chug, chug a lug
> Dig a hole, find a bug.

> (2) Lift it high, let it down
> Big machine eats the ground.
> Lift it high, let it down
> Big machine eats the ground

> (3) People watch and people cheer
> The big machine is coming near.
> People watch and people cheer
> The big machine is coming near.

Donaldson, Julia. *Stick Man.* Illustrated by Axel Scheffler. Scholastic, 2009. Ages 3–6.

Stick Man gets lost and is used for many different purposes before he is helped to find his way home. Ask: How many uses can you name for a 12-inch stick? Create silly sentences by choosing one item from each of the following lists.

small	stick man	hurried	along the beach
big	dog	spit	in the fireplace
mean	goose	waved	in the relay race
grumpy	man	rested	in the nest
pretty	Santa	sang	by the water

Gorbachev, Valeri. *Peter's Picture*. North-South Books, 2000. Ages 4–6.

Peter is proud of the picture he painted at school. He proudly carries it home, showing it to everyone he meets along the way. He receives many suggestions as to what to do with it, (smell it, give it to the bees, put it in a vase, water it) but his parents know exactly what to do with it, as Peter finds out. Ask: What ideas do you have for Peter's picture. Create a picture with shapes. Use large and small circles, squares, rectangles and triangles. For example, a cat can be created with a large circle for the body, a smaller circle for the head and two small triangles for the ears. Draw the eyes, mouth and tail.

Haan, Amanda. *I Call My Hand Gentle*. Illustrated by Marina Sagona. Viking, 2003. Ages 3–5.

Name things a hand can do: (pick, hug, throw, hold, pet, tickle, build, hammer, write, etc. Name things a hand should not do: steal, push, hurt, grab, break. Lead children through the following finger play:

TEN FINGERS (ANONYMOUS)

I have ten little fingers
And they belong to me.
I can make them do things.
Would you like to see?
I can shut them up tight
Or open them wide.
I can put them behind me and make them all hide.

Huxley, Aldous. *The Crows of Pearblossom*. Illustrated by Sophie Blackall. Abrams, 2011. Ages 5–8.

Mr. and Mrs. Crow live in a cottonwood tree. The hungry rattlesnake that lives at the bottom of the tree steals Mrs. Crow's eggs before they can hatch. Mr. Crow and his wise friend, Old Man Owl, come up with a plan to trick him. Ask: What do you suppose they will do? Here is information about crows. See how it is used in the song that follows. Use the information to add a different last line to the song.

Eat	*Are Found*	*Have*	*What they can do*
spiders	woods	black feathers	lay 5 eggs
eggs	fields	pointed bills	build nests

Sing to the tune of "Did You Ever See a Lassie?"

> *Did you ever see a black crow,*
> *A black crow, a black crow?*
> *Did you ever see a black crow,*
> *Eat spiders in the woods?*

Icenoggle, Jodi. *Till the Cows Come Home.* Illustrated by Normand Chartier. Boyds Mill, 2004. Ages 5–7.

Here is the western version of the traditional Jewish folktale. Ask: How many things can be made from a pair of chaps? The cowboy finds a way to use his chaps rather than throwing them away. This is called recycling. Three ways you can recycle are:

REUSE   RECYCLE   REFUSE

Name three things you can do.

I can recycle _____ by _____ instead
    of throwing it away.

I can recycle _____ by _____ instead
    of throwing it away.

I can recycle _____ by _____ instead
    of throwing it away.

Janowitz, Tama. *Hear That?* Illustrated by Tracy Dockray. Sea Star, 2011. Ages 3–5.

How many night noises can you name? A strange noise in the night has a mother and child looking for its source. They imagine all kinds of things the noise could be and are pleasantly surprised when they discover what it is. Play the poem "Louder Than" from Jack Prelutsky's recording of *New Kid on the Block* or read it aloud from the book. What other loud noises can children name? What quiet things can they name? Ask each child to draw a picture of something quiet. Put pictures together in a class "Quiet Book."

Laminack, Lester. *Three Hens and a Peacock*. Illustrated by Henry Cole. Peachtree Books, 2011. Ages 4–6.

The Tuckers' farm is a peaceful place. Cows chew their cuds. Hens lay their eggs and the old hound rests on the porch. Everyone has a job and no one complains. That is, until a peacock falls off the back of a passing truck and stirs things up.

Soon, customers are flocking to the farm to see what all the fuss is about and business is booming. But the hens don't like this newcomer getting attention while they stay cooped up doing all the hard work. The wise old hound sees the problem and helps his feathered friends orchestrate a job swap. What follows are three hens who get way in over their feathered heads and a distressed peacock who can't figure out how to lay an egg. Challenge children to complete these analogies about animals found in or around a farm.

Chicken is to egg and cow is to _____ (milk).

Rooster is to day as bat is to _____ (night).

Cat is to meow as dog is to _____ (bark).

Pig is to slop as horse is to _____ (hay).

Meng, Cece. *The Wonderful Thing About Hiccups*. Illustrated by Janet Peederson. Clarion Books. Ages 4–6.

The wonderful thing about hiccups, having a hippo, flying books, an ice cream party, belly bouncing — a hilarious tale with lots of imaginative connections. Ask children to come up with reasons that something not considered wonderful would be wonderful. Examples:

The wonderful thing about garbage is _____.

The wonderful thing about catching cold is _____.

The wonderful thing about thorns on a rosebush is _____.

Ask children to add more to the list.

Russell, Natalie. *Brown Rabbit in the City*. Viking, 2010. Ages 3–5.

How many things can you name that are found in a city? Brown Rabbit and his friend, Little Rabbit, rush from shop to cafe to art gallery, but what is the sight Brown Rabbit most wants to see?

Use the pattern below to describe the city as Brown Rabbit saw it.
If I sat on a hill in the country
I would hear birds singing
And I'd see children swimming in a pond
But I wouldn't hear elevated trains overhead
Or see people hurrying by
Because I'd see that in the city.

If I lived in the city _____
I would hear_____
And I'd see _____
But I wouldn't _____
Or_____
Because I'd see that in the country.

Taylor, Sean. *Huck Runs Amuck!* Illustrated by Peter Refolds. Dial, 2011. Ages 3–5.

Meet Huck. He loves flowers. And he'll do whatever it takes to get a mouthful; climb the highest mountain, walk a tightrope, even defy speeding trains. But when his mad dash up a church spire is mistaken for a heroic attempt to save Mrs. Spooner's flowery hat, Huck has a crisis of conscience. Play Clap It. Children clap the number of syllables in a flower name: rose, tulip, gardenia, chrysanthemum, daisy, violet, blue bonnet, orchid. Play Flower or Vegetable?

The leader names two vegetables and one flower in any order. Children clap when they hear the name of the flower.

Wahman, Wendy. *A Cat Like That.* Henry Holt, 2011. Ages 3–5.

What does a cat want in a best friend? Someone who can read the many moods of a cat's tail is what. Someone who knows when to play and when to stay away. Brainstorm what cats like and don't like then share the book. Play Catch the Clue. Read the clues one at a time until the children guess what the cat can do or all clues are read:

1. A cat can do it alone.
2. A cat can do it with other cats.
3. A cat does not need anything to do it.
4. It does not cost money to do this.
5. Dogs cannot do it.

6. A cat can do it on the porch or in the tree.
7. A cat can do it at night or during the day.
8. A cat will not do it on command.
9. Birds cannot learn to do it.
10. Sound is an important part of this activity. (Answer: Meow)

FIVE

Developing Analytical/ Mathematical Thinking

Analytical Thinking

Before drawing conclusions or making decisions, the analytical thinker examines the facts and makes predictions as to outcomes based on evidence. The analytical thinker is organized and is concerned with relationships — how things work together or complement each other and how things are constructed.

The analytical thinker looks for similarities and differences in both concrete materials and in situations. They plan ahead by determining the steps to be taken in a task, the materials needed and the problems that might be encountered.

The analytical thinker is adept at forecasting or making predictions based on evidence. Encouraging predictions at story time for the youngest child will help the child toward academic success in years to come. Kenneth Goodman, in Theoretical Models and Processes of Reading (IRA 1970), says, "Good thinkers and readers are good predictors. The proficient reader uses the least amount of information to make the best possible guesses."

YOUNG CHILDREN ANALYZE

Is This a House for Hermit Crab? by Megan McDonald.

Hermit Crab is looking for a new home. Scritch, scratch he goes along the shore, by the sea, in the sand. But each home he finds has something wrong with it. To determine the suitability of each new home, children must be aware of the size of Hermit Crab and of the attributes of each home Hermit Crab tries. Why would these homes be inappropriate? A large rock, a tin can, a bucket, a hollow log, a fishing net?

Analyzing Vocabulary

Before hearing a book talk about Sylvester the donkey and group these words, which will be in the story. Put an *F* before feelings, a *T* before things, and a *D* before words that describe. Work with a partner or group. Guess if you do not know a word. This activity can be done orally as a group

1. ____ pebbles	4. ____ remarkable	7. ____ extraordinary
2. ____ gully	5. ____ puzzled	8. ____ bewildered
3. ____ alfalfa	6. ____ sassafras	9. ____ perplexed

Share *Sylvester and the Magic Pebble* by William Steig.

Sylvester Duncan, a young donkey, lives with his mother and father. One of his hobbies is collecting <u>pebbles</u>. One day, searching in a <u>gully</u>, he finds a <u>remarkable</u> red pebble with <u>extraordinary</u> powers. As he rushes home to show it to his parents, he is frightened by a lion and immediately wishes to become a stone. His wish is granted and the lion wanders off <u>bewildered</u>, <u>puzzled</u> and <u>perplexed</u>. When the pebble rolls away from the stone (Sylvester), Sylvester cannot wish to become himself again. His sad parents remain at home drinking <u>sassafras</u> tea and saving the best <u>alfalfa</u> for their son's return. The story ends with a happy reunion of Sylvester and his parents.

PREDICTIVE QUESTIONING

Predictive questioning is the natural way to approach literature. The typical adult does not finish a novel and then proceed to ask questions about who was in the story or where the story took place. These questions come before reading, not after. It is the anticipation and guessing of what will happen next that keeps the reader reading. In reading aloud and talking about books, you can help the child to analyze what is read by the questions you ask:

1. Forecasting: Given what has happened in the story, predict what will happen next. How do you think the story will end?

2. Cause and effect: If _____ happens, what will be the result?

3. Reorganization: If the _____ in the story were a _____ how would the story be different?

4. Analysis: How is this story like another story we have read?

   How is this character like a character in a different story?

   How are the two characters alike?

It is important to note that close observation and the ability to analyze a situation or problem go hand in hand. Because the images on television change rapidly, the child cannot experience close observation of the images. Picture books can provide this experience. Allow the child plenty of time to study the illustrations before responding to analysis questions. In a fine picture book the illustrations bring an added dimension to the text, they do not simply duplicate the text.

Excellent picture books to help young readers develop analytical skills are the easy-to-read mysteries of Crosby Bonsall or Marjorie Sharmat . An introduction to these delightful books follows:

MYSTERIES FOR THE YOUNGEST READER

The leader can introduce these authors to young readers with the short paragraphs shown. Here are five mystery books for you to read by the famous author Crosby Bonsall. The last line of each verse is the title of one of the books. Sing the songs. Find the books in your library. Solve the mysteries! (Tune: "Farmer in the Dell")

> *A cat disappears.*
> *Go and find her now.*
> *Who can solve the mystery of*
> The Case of the Cat's Meow?

> *With messages in code and*
> *A bearded man who's boss,*
> *Who can solve the mystery of*
> The Case of the Double Cross?

When bathtubs overflow
And doorbells ring pell mell,
Who can solve the mystery of
The Case of the Dumb Bells?

Mrs. Meech has lost her pie.
The dog hides in the manger
Who can solve the mystery of
The Case of the Hungry Stranger?

Can girls solve a crime?
Do boys get all the pats?
Who can solve the mystery of
The Case of the Scaredy Cats?

The leader says: "Here are four mystery books for you (or to have read to you) to read by the famous author Marjorie Sharmat. The last line of each verse is the title of one of the books. Find the books in your library. Solve the mysteries!"

The paper it was gone,
The paper it was missed.
Can you solve the mystery of
Nate the Great and the Lost List?

Hex the cat is missing.
Who would pull such a stunt?
Can you solve the mystery of
Nate the Great and the Halloween Hunt?

On the ballfield something
Wasn't in its place.
Can you solve the mystery of
Nate the Great and the Stolen Base?

It didn't have a label,
It didn't have a tag.
Can you solve the mystery of
Nate the Great and the Boring Beach Bag?

QUESTIONS TO ASK
FOR ANALYTICAL THINKING

1. What was the problem in the story?
2. Who or what do you think caused the problem?
3. How is this story like another story we have shared?
   • How are the settings alike and different?
   • How are the characters alike and different?
4. How many other ways might the problem have been solved?
5. After _____what do you think will happen next?

BOOKS AND ACTIVITIES
FOR ANALYTICAL THINKING

Brett, Jan. *Annie and the Wild Animals*. Houghton Mifflin, 1995. Ages 4–6.

It has been a long winter and the snow is falling again. Annie and her cat, Taffy stay warm and dry in a cozy cottage. Then one morning Annie cannot find Taffy anywhere. Before Taffy disappeared she had been acting strangely. Annie wonders what was the matter. Annie waits for Taffy to return but no matter how long she waits and watches, Taffy is not to be seen. So Annie decides to make some corn cakes and leave them at the edge of the woods to attract another small animal to be her pet. Annie cannot believe the animals that appear — a moose, a wildcat, a bear and a stag. None of these animals would make a good pet. They snarl and roar even louder when Annie runs out of corn meal and had no corn cakes to give them. What will Annie do?

Brett, Jan. *Berlioz the Bear*. G.P. Putnam's Sons, 1991. Ages 4–6.

Suppose you are asked to play at a ball. Suppose you are asked to bring the entire orchestra. Suppose you have trouble getting to the ball. That is what happens to Berlioz. First, he hears a strange noise in his double bass. It doesn't sound like music at all. Next, after all the players climb in the wagon, the wheel gets stuck in a hole. None of the musicians can pull the wagon out of the hole. How can they get to the ballroom on time?

Add the missing rhyming words.

1. I had a bear and his name was Howl.

   I don't know why but he loved to g_____.

2. I had a rooster and his name was Moe.

   I don't know why but he loved to c_____.

3. I had a cat and her name was Gurr.

   I don't know why but she loved to p_____.

4. I had a dog and his name was Sap.

   I don't know why but he loved to y_____.

5. I had a goat and her name was Fleet.

   I don't know why but she loved to bl_____.

Burton, Virginia Lee. *Mike Mulligan and His Steam Shovel.* Houghton Mifflin, 1967. Ages 4–6.

Mike Mulligan and his steam shovel, Mary Anne, have worked together for many years. They dig canals, tunnels and roadways. Mike brags that Mary Anne can dig as much in a day as one hundred men could dig in a week. The two are put to the test and asked to dig a basement for the Town Hall. Mike and Mary Anne are so busy digging that they forget to plan how to get out of the large hole. Then a young boy thinks of a perfect solution. What can be done?

Divide into three groups. Group one chants the first verse three times. After group one chants the verse once, group two begins to chant verse two and chants it two times. After group two chants its verse one time, group three chants its verse. All should end at the same time.

(1) Chug, chug. chug a lug,
   Dig a hole, find a bug.
   Chug, chug, chug a lug,
   Dig a hole, find a bug.

(2) Lift it high, let it down.
   Mary Anne eats the ground.
   Lift it high, let it down.
   Mary Anne eats the ground.

(3) People watch and people cheer.
   A new Town Hall is coming here.

People watch and people cheer.
A new Town Hall is coming here.

Clifford, Eth. *Flatfoot Fox and the Case of the Missing Eye.* Illustrated by Brian Lies. Houghton Mifflin, 1990.

Flatfoot Fox, the smartest detective in the world, is sitting in his office, just waiting for something to happen, when in walks Fat Cat. Fat Cat is mean and Fat Cat is mad — and what's more, Fat Cat has a mystery to be solved. Detective Fox and his faithful assistant, Secretary Bird, set out to discover who has been the thief at Fat Cat's birthday party. Flatfoot Fox finds the culprit in true detective style, of course, but before the case is closed the two have met a zany assortment of suspects, starting with a Really Ridiculous Rabbit. Flatfoot Fox proves how clever he is. Can you solve the mystery before Flatfoot Fox does?

dePaola, Tomie. *Strega Nona.* Scholastic, 1975. Reissue 2010. Ages 4–6.

In the town of Calabria, there lives an old lady everyone calls Strega Nona, which means "Grandma Witch." The town would go to see her if they had troubles. Since Strega Nona is getting old she needs help. So she puts up a help-wanted sign in the town square. Big Anthony, who doesn't pay attention, goes to see her and starts working for Strega Nona. But there is one condition — he must never touch her cooking pot. However, in her absence he says the magic words that cause the pot to cook. Pasta is everywhere! Unfortunately, Big Anthony does not know the words to turn the pot off. Imagine what happens when Strega Nona returns!

Play the I Have/Who Has Game. Cut the cards apart and give one card to each of five players. The player with the *** on their card begins with the question. The player with the answer reads the answer, then their question.

I HAVE: Strega Nona stopped the pot from cooking.
[***Start Here]
WHO HAS: What did Strega Nona have?

I HAVE: Strega Nona had a magic cooking pot.
WHO HAS: What did Big Anthony do?

I HAVE: Big Anthony told the pot to start cooking.
WHO HAS: What did the people of the town do?

I HAVE: The people of the town ate the pasta until they
were full.
WHO HAS: Why could Big Anthony not stop the pot
from cooking?

I HAVE: He did not know to blow three kisses to the pot.
WHO HAS: What did Strega Nona do?

---

dePaola, Tomie. *Strega Nona's Harvest*. G.P. Putnam's Sons, 2009.
Ages 4–5.

While Strega Nona's garden is just perfect, Big Anthony's garden
turns out to be a jungle. What will they do with all of these vegetables?
Ask children to describe a vegetable by using a word that begins with
the same letter as the vegetable. Example: Crunchy carrots or lovely
lettuce.

Gag, Wanda. *Millions of Cats*. Coward-McCann, 1928. Ages 4–6.

A little old man and a little old woman are lonely so they decide
that a cat is just what they need for company. The little old man sets
out to find a cat, walking through cool valleys until he comes to a hill
covered with cats. There are "Hundreds of cats, thousands of cats,
millions and billions and trillions of cats" and every single one of them
follows him home. Now the old couple know they cannot possibly
feed all of the cats. What should they do?

Hassett, Ann. *Too Many Frogs*. Illustrated by John Hassett. Houghton Mifflin, 2011. Ages 4–6.

Nana Quimby has a problem. Frogs come up from her basement
while she is trying to bake a cake. But the thumping, bumping, and
banging become too much to ignore. How can she get rid of too many
frogs?

Solve the problem of too many cats or too many frogs by using this
problem solving model. List and score three ideas. 1=no 3=maybe
3=yes

List your ideas   Fast   Low cost   Will work   Total

_____

_____

_____

Henkes, Kevin. *Chrysanthemum.* Greenwillow, 2000. Ages 4–6.

Because her parents thought she was an absolutely perfect baby they gave her a very special name, Chrysanthemum. But going to school for the first time is a shock. The other children make fun of her name. They say it is too long and will not fit on her name tag. They say she is a flower to be picked and smelled. Each day Chrysanthemum takes longer and longer to get to school. What can Chrysanthemum do to keep the children from laughing at her? Imagine you are Chrysanthemum's best friend. What could you do to help her?

Hulbert, Laura. *Too Many Feet.* Illustrated by Erik Brooks. Henry Holt, 2011. Ages 3–6.

In a lively guessing game, find out why the feet of tree frogs and those of eight other animals are perfectly adapted to their habitats.

Juster, Norton. *The Odious Ogre.* Illustrated by Jules Feiffer. Scholastic, 2011. Ages 4–6.

A rotten, angry, hungry ogre terrorizes the town and dines on its hapless citizens. Nothing can stop him until he meets a kind and friendly young lady. What so you think she does? (Sing this song to the tune of "The Farmer in the Dell.")

> *An ogre's in the meadow,*
> *An ogre's in the meadow,*
> *Stomping, roaring, making noise*
> *An ogre's in the meadow*

Change the lines to tell other things the ogre did.

McCloskey, Robert. *Make Way for Ducklings.* Viking, 1999. Ages 4–6.

"Look out!" squawks Mrs. Mallard. "You'll get run over!" The Public Garden, in Boston, is a dangerous place to raise a family of ducklings, so the search begins for a new home. Mr. and Mrs. Mallard fly over Beacon Hill, around the State House, and through Louisburg

Square to find a better place for hatching ducklings. What do you think will make a good home for a duck family? Read the poem and at your signal the children respond "quack, quack, quack."

> A mother duck cried
> Quack, quack, quack.
> She told her ducklings
> Come back come back.
> The little ducklings said
> Quack, quack, quack,
> We've found a home
> In a tall haystack.

Nolan, Jerdine. *Hewitt Anderson's Great Big Life*. Illustrated by Kadie Nelson. Simon & Schuster, 2005. Ages 4–6.

Hewitt is sweet, smart and polite but very tiny, and his parents are giants. How can he manage to live in a world of big things? Ask the children to fill in the missing words. What other problems might a tiny person have in a big world?

> Poor Hewitt Anderson was, oh, so small.
> He measured on a ruler only two (1) i _____ tall.
> He had trouble turning (2) l _____both off and on,
> And he couldn't wash the (3) d _____ or mow the (4) l
> _____.

Answers: 1. inches 2. lights 3. dishes 4. lawn

Polette, Keith. *Isabelle and the Hungry Coyote*. Illustrated by Esther Szegedy. Raven Tree Press, 2004. Ages 5–8.

How can Isabelle take goodies to her grandmother when the coyote gets to grandmother's cottage first? There is no hunter to save her. What will she do when coyote tries to eat her up? As Isabelle walks through the desert to her Abuela's casa, here are sights she sees:

> On the first day of spring,
> What did I see but a cactus flower
> Waving at me.
>
> On the second day of spring,
> What did I see but a rattlesnake
> Rattling at me.

On the third day of spring,
What did I see but a prairie dog
Peeking at me.

On the fourth day of spring,
What did I see but a tumbleweed
Tumbling at me.

On the fifth day of spring
What did I see but Abuela
Baking for me.

Rubin, Adam. *Those Darn Squirrels and the Cat Next Door*. Illustrated by Daniel Salmieri. Houghton Mifflin, 2011. Ages 4–6.

Muffins, the cat, terrorizes the birds and ties the squirrels' tails together. What can the squirrels do to put a stop to Muffins' bad behavior? Add the missing words to each last line of the Friendship Song (tune: "The Bear Went Over the Mountain").

> *What can you do with a good friend?*
> *What can you do with a good friend?*
> *What can you do with a good friend?*
> *It's a word that rhymes with ring (sing).*
> *It's a word that rhymes with day (play).*
> *It's a word that rhymes with meet (eat).*

What other words can children add?

Sharmat, Marjorie. *Nate the Great and the Sticky Case*. Coward-McCann, 1998. Ages 5–7.

Nate the Great (detective) is asked to find something big on something small. Claude is the one who has lost it. Can you guess what it is? Claude has a stamp collection and he has lost his stegosaurus stamp. Nate knows that finding a stamp will not be easy but he is up to the task. He questions friends who were at Claude's house and who were looking at his stamps. Then the rain which has stopped, gives him a sticky idea until he follows the trail of the sticky stamp. Can you find the stamp before Nate does?

Small, David. *Imogene's Antlers*. Crown, 1995. Ages 4–6.

Suppose you woke up one morning to discover you had acquired part of an animal! This is what happens to Imogene when she awakens to find she has sprouted antlers. They do cause some difficulty for her in getting dressed and going through doors. Her mother's reaction at the sight of her daughter with antlers is to faint. None of the experts consulted can help Imogene but she does discover that antlers have some useful purposes. How many can you think of? Let's Do Math!

1. Imogene dried three towels on her antlers. Lucy brought her two more to dry. How many towels did Imogene dry? _____

2. Imogene had six donuts on her antlers. Two hungry birds each took a donut. How many donuts are on her antlers now?

3. Imogene shared two peacock feathers with two friends. How many feathers did she share in all?

Thompson, Lauren. *Mouse's First Spring*. Illustrated by Burket Erdogan. Simon & Schuster, 2005. Ages 3–5.

A fun guessing book as mouse discovers signs of spring. Have children make up spring riddles. Each riddle should have three clues. The last word of the third clue should rhyme with the answer to the riddle, for example:

1. It comes in many colors.
2. It is found in meadows and gardens.
3. Its name rhymes with hour.

Tompert, Ann. *The Pied Piper of Peru*. Illustrated by Kestuti Kasparavicius. Boyds Mill, 2002. Ages 4–6.

When Brother Martin is ordered to set traps and put out poison to rid the priory of mice, he knows he can't harm the creatures. Neither can he disobey an order from his superior. It is when he meet a brave mouse that they find a solution to the problem. What do you suppose they do? Answer some mice riddles:

Well behaved mice are (nice mice).
Mice that do things two times are (twice mice).

Cold mice are (ice mice).
Mice that tell others what to do are (advice mice).

Weigelt, Udo. *Who Stole the Gold?* Illustrated by Julia Gukovva. North-South Books, 2000. Ages 4–6.

Can you find which of the forest suspects is guilty when Hamster finds his gold is missing? Follow the clues!

Play the Animal Story Game (tune: "Farmer in the Dell"). Children sing:

> *What story did we read?*
> *What story did we read?*
> *A rabbit hid in a watering can.*
> *What story did we read? (Peter Rabbit)*

Ask how may ways we can change the third line.
More ideas for the third line:

> *A big bad wolf blew a stick house down (Three Little Pigs)*
> *A little girl broke a chair (Goldilocks)*
> *A spider spins wonderful words in her web (Charlotte's Web)*

Wood, Audrey, *Heckedy Peg.* Illustrated by Don Wood. Harcourt Brace Jovonovich, 1997. Ages 5–8.

A mother has seven children named Monday, Tuesday, Wednesday, Thursday, Friday, Saturday and Sunday. She goes into town promising to bring each child a gift if they will not let strangers into the house or play with fire. The children forget her warnings when Heckedy Peg offers them gold to let her in and light her pipe. She turns each child into a food, puts the food in her sack and takes them with her. When the mother, who arrives home, is told by a little bird what happened, she sets off to rescue her children. The only way she can do this is to guess which food each child has become. Do you think she can do it? Can you?

Activity: Ask the children to close their eyes after hearing the story: Picture a good witch. Remember, she doesn't have to be beautiful to be good. Now think of a good name for your witch. She must have something magic in her house and a good spell. Tell the group her name and her spell.

Mathematical Thinking

Closely related to convergent/analytical thinking is logical/mathematical thinking. Both require the ability to see relationships, or how things fit together, as well as the ability to compare and contrast relevant bits of information.

Logical/mathematical thinkers do well with activities that involve linear thinking including the following:

Sequencing
Predicting
Measuring
Logic games
Solving puzzles
Classifying
Working with shapes.

SEQUENCE AND TIME

The Grouchy Ladybug by Eric Carle.

A grouchy ladybug looking for a fight meets a friendly ladybug, a yellow jacket, a praying mantis, a stag beetle, a sparrow, a lobster, a skunk, a boa constrictor, a hyena, a gorilla, a rhinoceros, and an elephant and offers to fight each one. She finally meets her match when a whale's tail gives her a slap, sending her back to where she started.

Let each child choose the part they want to be and have them line up in the order each appears in the story.

Play: What Time Is It? (Use a clock with movable hands.)

1. The story begins at six o'clock in the morning. One hour later the ladybug meets stag beetle. What time is it? _____

2. At nine o'clock, ladybug meets a sparrow. One hour earlier she spoke to a praying mantis. What time did she speak to the praying mantis? _____

3. At ten o'clock she meets a lobster. Two hours later she meets a boa constrictor. At what time did she see the boa constrictor? _____

4. At three o'clock she sees a rhinoceros. Two hours later she meets a whale. What time did she meet the whale? _____

COUNTING RHYMES

Children hold up fingers when they hear a number in this rhyme.

> Hickory, dickory dot,
> One mouse climbed in a pot.
> Don't stop to gawk,
> Here comes a hawk,
> Hickory, dickory dot.
>
> Hickory, dickory dill,
> Two mice stood very still,
> Don't be dull,
> Here comes a gull,
> Hickory, dickory dill.
>
> Hickory, dickory dee,
> Three mice climbed up a tree,
> And then cried "Foul!"
> Here comes an owl,
> Hickory, dickory dee.
>
> Hickory, dickory dole,
> Four mice hid in a hole.
> Then wouldn't you know,
> Here comes a crow,
> Hickory, dickory dole.
>
> Hickory, dickory day,
> It's time to run away.
> So pack your trunk,
> Here comes a skunk,
> Hickory, dickory day!

BOOKS AND ACTIVITIES FOR LOGICAL MATHEMATICAL THINKING

1. Counting

Begin with any five items — pennies, chairs, fingers, children. Bounce a ball and have the child count the number of bounces. When 1–5 has been mastered go to 6–10.

2. Questions about Size

Show books about shoes, hands, a cow, a mouse. Ask the children to:

Name something smaller than your shoe.
Name something larger than your hand.
Name something larger than a cow.
Name something smaller than a mouse.

Pass out picture books about animals. Ask each child to name something smaller and larger than the animal on the cover of their book.

3. Questions about Wide and Narrow

Ask the following questions:

What is wider than your book?
What is narrower than your book?
What is longer your pencil?
What is shorter than a ruler?

4. Ordering Activity

Collect eight books of different sizes. Ask the children to line them up from tallest to shortest, largest to smallest. etc.

Collect eight books with individual animals on the cover. Can the child group the books by the shortest and tallest animals? Smallest and largest animals? How else might the books be grouped?

5. What animals can children name that have patterns on their skin?

6. What stories can children name that have three characters in them?

7. How many pairs of items can children name that go together? Have them explain why.

8. Challenge a group of children to make circles, triangles and squares with their bodies.

Albee, Sarah. *The Dragon's Scales.* Illustrated by John Manders. Random House, 2004. Ages 5–7.

The dragon won't let people cross the bridge to get to the berry patches until a math contest using the dragon's scales is proposed and won by a little girl.

A fun read-aloud.

Activity: Have some imaginary fun. Bring out a carefully wrapped box and gently unwrap it. Reach into the box and holding out your empty hand give each child an imaginary dragon's egg. Tell the children to find a hiding place for their egg until it is time for it to hatch. Each child can imagine the color of his own egg and what might be inside it. At hatching time let each child tell what was inside his egg.

Anderson, Lena. *Ten for Tea.* R & S Books, 2000. Ages 4–6.

A delightful counting book that begins with Hedgehog at home waiting for visitors so she won't be "just one." Uncle Will arrives, making two, followed by Elephant, Duck, Teddy and a host of others to make ten, all sitting around Hedgehog's table drinking tea and eating cookies. Suppose Hedgehog had ten cookies and five visitors. How many would each visitor get? Ask more questions related to the number of visitors and the number of cookies.

Ashburn, Boni. *Over at the Castle.* Illustrated by Kelly Murphy. Abrams, 2010. Ages 4–6.

A delightful counting story that introduces all the workers in a castle watched over by two eager dragons. Have the children take the parts of the workers in the castle and line up in the order each appeared in the story. Let each child tell what she thinks her job would be in the castle.

Base, Graeme. *Uno's Garden.* Abrams, 2006. All ages.

A story book, puzzle book and numbers book that makes a plea for the environment.

Play the Flower Game: Put names of flowers on separate slips of paper in a box. Each player chooses one name. The first player goes to the chalkboard and puts the letter *X* in place of the letters in the name, for example: XXXX (for ROSE). The player calls on another in the group to guess a letter. Example: The third *X* is the letter *S*. If this is correct the student can try to guess the flower. If the guess is correct, that student comes to the board and puts *X*s for his flower name. If either guess is not correct, another student is called upon to guess.

Butler, John. *Ten in the Den*. Peachtree, 2005. Ages 3–5.

A delightful counting book. Ten sleepy animals disappear one by one so that little mouse can sleep. When mouse is all alone he misses his friends. Activity: Count the number of friends as each arrives and as each departs.

Noisy friends bothered mouse. Talk with children about other habits that annoy people. Point out that habits can change and ask children to give examples of things they used to do that they no longer do.

Cuyler, Margery. *Guinea Pigs Add Up*. Illustrated by Tracey Pearson. Walker, 2011. Ages 4–6.

Here is a classroom with a problem. Guinea pigs keep adding and adding. From one lonely guinea pig to two to five and all the way up to twenty! The kids find that having a classroom pet is more than they bargained for. Finally each student gets to take a guinea pig home, until they are left with zero — that is, until Mr. Gilbert brings in a rabbit with a growing belly.

Propose simple subtraction problems. If we have six guinea pigs and five children each take one home, how many are left?

Fox, Mem. *Counting Goats*. Illustrated by Jan Thomas. Simon & Schuster, 2010. Ages 3–5.

Here are goats of all shapes, sizes, hobbies and professions that can be counted on each page. Share *The Three Billy Goats Gruff*. How many other tales can children name that have the number three in the title?

Jansson, Tove. *Moomin's Little Book of Numbers*. Farrar, Straus & Giroux, 2011. Ages 2–3.

Moomin troll, Moominmama and Snork Maiden create a game out of learning to count from one to ten with every day objects such as seashells and stars. A board book. Count objects on each page with the child.

Schnur, Steven. *Night Lights.* Illustrated by Stacey Schuett. Farrar, Straus & Giroux, 2000. Ages 4–6.

A little girl counts one light in her room, two amber blinking clocks, four candles and finally the night sky with a million stars. Create a 1–10 counting book using objects found in a house, for example: One refrigerator, two rugs, three mirrors....

Shields, Carol. *Wombat Walkabout.* Illustrated by Sophie Blackall. Dutton, 2009. Ages 6–8.

A counting poem with six wombats on a trip through the Australian outback. Activity: Find Australia on a map. What direction is it from the U.S.? Share *Koala Lou* by Mem Fox. Show books with Australian animals on the cover. Help children identify each animal. Sing this Australia animal song to the tune of "Waltzing Matilda."

> *Here come the wombats,*
> *Here come the 'gators,*
> *Here come the koala bears,*
> *All in a row.*
> *Wombats,*
> *Alligators,*
> *Furry, furry koala bears,*
> *Australian animals*
> *That we should know.*

Singer, Marilyn. *Quiet Night.* Illustrated by John Manders. Clarion, 2002, Ages 3–5.

A counting book that allows children to make the night sounds of various animals — a fun participation story. Ask children to add verses to this poem that tell what a turtle, a rabbit and a deer would eat and how they would leave (hopped away? ran away? crawled away?)

> A fish swam in a quiet pond
> All on a summer's day
> What to eat? What to eat?
> She nibbled a worm and swam away.
>
> A deer _____by a quiet pond
> All on a summer's day.

What to eat? What to eat?

He _____ some _____ and ___ away.

Van Laan, Nancy. *A Tree for Me.* Illustrated by Sheila Stanton. Knopf, 2000. Ages 5–7.

Big one? Small One? Skinny one? Tall one? Which tree will be a perfect one for a small child to climb? This book is filled with animals to count, sounds to imitate and patterns to repeat.

Share this story and puzzle:

There once was a tree that sang when the wind blew. Pierre, the woodcutter, said, "A tree that makes a beautiful song will make a beautiful clock. I will cut it down."

The people of the town told Pierre he must find another tree. He could not cut down the tree that makes a beautiful song. But Pierre knew that no other tree would do. His clock must come from the beautiful singing tree.

How can Pierre make this happen without cutting down the tree? Think of many ideas.

Walsh, Ellen. *Balancing Act.* Simon & Schuster, 2011. Ages 2–5.

Two mice make a teeter-totter. They are balancing just fine when along comes a frog. Can they make room for one more friend? What about two? What about more? Then a big bird comes along and wants to play, too. What will happen now?

Activity: The mice in this story had many friends. List the letters of the word friend vertically on the board. Ask children to choose a word that begins with each letter and then agree that it is a characteristic of a friend.

F aithful

R eliable

I nteresting

E arnest

N eighborly

D ecent

SIX

Developing Visual Literacy

What Is Visual Literacy?

How often have you watched a young child take apart a toy piece by piece or construct a variety of objects from Legos or Lincoln Logs? This same child will enjoy jigsaw puzzles and often will choose puzzles to work that are intended for a much older person. This is the visually aware child, who sees how things go together in ways that others might miss. Some have labeled these children "art smart." They often communicate more effectively visually than verbally.

Certainly perception and awareness are key components in the development of color, shadings, light contrasts, figures, patterns and detail. Numerous picture books highlight these components. One such book is Joan Steiner's *Look Alikes*, which encourages children to examine details carefully to find hidden objects as well as to spot likenesses and differences in the images presented.

Young children should be introduced to the concept books of Tana Hoban, who, through marvelous photography, helps the child to identify and contrast items by shape, size, texture and pattern. Among her titles to be shared are *Count and See*; *Cubes, Cones, Cylinders and Spheres*; *Exactly the Opposite*; *Is It Larger? Is It Smaller?*; *Shadow and Reflections* and *Shapes, Shapes, Shapes*.

The visually literate person understands how messages and moods are communicated through art. They are able to interpret action in illustration, react verbally to visual work, read simple body language and identify work which communicates specific mood. Among the many fine wordless picture books open to multiple interpretation are David Wiesner's *Tuesday* and *Flotsam* and Ezra Jack Keats' *Clementina's Cactus*. Very young children will enjoy interpreting the action in Jerry Pinkney's *Lion and the Mouse*.

The visually literate person can identify simple symbols and their meaning and can verbalize the meanings of symbols used in place of words. The preschool/kindergarten child will shiver with delight in "reading" Alyssa Capucilli's *Inside a House That Is Haunted*, in which she substitutes pictures for words. None of the previously mentioned visual skills occur in isolation. The eyes and the brain must work together to deal with given information.

LOOKING AT AN ILLUSTRATION

Questions to ask when a child is looking at an illustration could include the following:

1. What kinds of lines do you see?

2. Are there more straight lines or curved lines?

3. Is this a very busy picture or a quiet picture? How do you know?

4. What is a picture frame? Is something framed in this picture?

5. What is the largest thing in the picture? The smallest? Do you think the largest thing might be most important to the story?

6. What colors make you feel happy? Sad? Fearful?

7. What colors has the artist used? What mood do the colors create?

8. Do you like this picture? Why or why not?

9. After looking at this picture, predict what will happen next.

ACTIVITIES TO DEVELOP VISUAL LITERACY

1. Make available for cut out different shapes: squares, rectangles, triangles and circles of various sizes. Ask the children to create images by combining these shapes. For example, a witch can have a large triangle for the body, smaller triangle arms and legs, a circle face and a triangle hat. Characters created can also be animals.

2. Holiday placemats. Have children draw holiday symbols or a holiday picture on a 9 × 12 sheet of construction paper. Use blunt scissors to fringe the edges for a holiday place mat.

3. Paper plates can become puppets when folded in half and glued to a tongue depressor. The face is then drawn on the half plate.

4. Find pictures related to the same topic (farm, circus, etc.) Allow children time to look at the pictures. Choose a child to close her eyes. Take away a picture to see if the child can tell which one is missing.

5. Play Who Ran Away?

Gather six to eight books, each with a cover picture of a different animal. Allow the child/ren one minute to look at the covers. Children then close their eyes while one book is removed. Ask: "Which animal ran away?" Continue the game by removing two books, then three. Once children see how the game works they will observe more closely.

6. Show covers of books that feature the same fairy tale character (all witches, all giants, all princesses, etc.). Ask: Which _____ do you like best? Why?

7. Play Watch My Fingers (anonymous)
I have ten moving fingers [hold up both hands, wiggle fingers].
As busy as can be.
Here are thing that they can do
Watch my hands and see.
I can shut them up tight [make a fist].
Or open them wide [stretch open].
I can put them together [clasp hands].
Or make them all hide [put hands behind back].
I can make them jump high [stretch arms above head].
I can make them jump low [put hands below waist].
I can fold them quietly [fold as if in prayer].
And hold them just so [shake hands with another child].

8. Visualizing Letters
The leader spells the name of a fairy tale character. Children raise their hands above their heads if the letter extends above the line (example: *t*). They drop their hands below their waists if the letter extends below the line (example: *g*). They put their hands on their hips if the letter rests on the line (example: *a*)

9. Share a familiar tale where the main character undertakes a journey.

Examples are *Little Red Riding Hood* or *Goldilocks and the Three Bears*. Ask the child/ren to draw a map of the journey.

10. Using play dough, children create animals after forming the dough into squares, circles and triangles.

11. Create opposites by folding a paper in half and drawing on each side of the paper something that is big/little, tall/short, wide/narrow, over/under. What other opposites can children name and draw?

12. Share Anno's *Upside-Downers*, where, in the land of cards, everyone has an upside-down double. The text can be read upside down or downside-up or by two children at once facing each other.

13. Visualize: Suppose there was nothing red in the world. What would be missing? Do the same for green or blue or any other color.

14. Use old magazines to create collages centered around the picture book that has been shared. For example, after sharing *Joseph Had a Little Overcoat*, create a collage of items that could be recycled.

15. Children draw and color pictures of a colorful meal. Each item in the meal is a different color.

16. Share the many delightful books written and illustrated by Jan Brett. Visit Jan Brett's Web site, www.janbrett.com, for a wide variety of art activities, including alphabet coloring pages, bookmarks, calendars, character masks, borders, holiday crafts and cards and much more.

BOOKS AND ACTIVITIES FOR VISUAL LITERACY

Anno, Mitsumasa. *Topsy Turvies*. Philomel, 1989. Ages 4–8.

In this wordless picture book is a topsy-turvy world where anything is possible. Elf-like men swim in a book, suspend from underneath a staircase, hang a picture on the floor and dive off a playing card. Which is up and which is down? What is front and what is back? Where is top and where is bottom? Show a busy picture. Ask: How many "betweens" can you find? Children respond by telling how one object is between two other objects. Continue by asking about other positions: over, under, on, above, below.

Base, Graeme. *Animalia.* Abrams, 1989. Ages 6–12.

As you travel from A to Z, the details on each new page begin with the letter for that page. Thus, *H* is for Horrible Hairy Hogs. You will also find hamsters and hang gliders, hippos and hummingbirds, hammocks and horses. The author as a boy is hiding in each illustration. Choose any letter of the alphabet. Find that page in the book. Name all the things on the page that begin with that letter. Older children can create alliterative sentences using items on the page. Example: Heavy hippos have huge horses.

Chedru, Delphine. *Spot It Again!* Abrams, 2011. Ages 3–5.

Surprises and secrets fill the pages as young readers are asked to look carefully at a series of patterns and layouts. On every page there are hidden creatures. Some are embedded in the design and some can be found underneath flaps. Readers will search until have found every one.

Activity: Hidden Pictures: Many daily papers have look alike drawings which challenge the viewer to find the differences. Share also the hidden pictures in current and back issues of *Highlights Magazine.*

Cocagne, Marie-Pascale. *The Big Book of Shapes.* Illustrated by Bridget Strevens-Marzo. Abrams 2010. Ages 3–5.

This activity book allows readers to create their own colorful world out of squares, circles and triangles. The large format and spiral binding make it easy to use. Challenge children to create people or animals using only squares, circles and triangles.

Fox, Paula. *Traces.* Illustrated by Karla Kuskin. Boyds Mill, 2011. Ages 4–6.

"What leaves bubbles of water and air on a lily pond? What leaves a path across the sand into the sea? What leaves shadows on the ground?" These questions and more are raised and answered in this quiet exploration of the traces different creatures and things leave behind as they go on their way,

Activity: Take a nature walk in a park or the woods. How many "Traces" can you find? On a warm day watch for an anthill. Share this verse and see which parts of the verse the children observe.

Come and see the busy ants.
The ants are having fun.
The worker ants bring in the food
Enough for everyone.
The soldier ants crack open seeds
And give them to the Queen.
The little ants care for the young
And keep things neat and clean.

Frazier, Craig. *Bee and Bird.* Roaring Brook Press, 2011. Ages 4–6.

The first page shows a series of black and yellow alternating stripes. What is it? Turn the page to find the body of a bee. Where is the bee? Turn the page and find the bee on the back of Bird. More surprises take place as Bee and Bird make their way from a tree to a truck to a cow in this wordless book.

Activity: Make your own bird using a large circle for the body, a smaller circle for the head and a triangle for the beak. Paste on construction paper and draw an eye and legs. Draw feathers on your bird. Add anything else you wish in order to make this your special bird.

Hall, Zoe. *Fall Leaves Fall.* Illustrated by Shari Halpern. Scholastic, 2000. Ages 3–5.

A delightful look at leaves, all sizes, shapes and colors.

Activity: Bring in a collection of leaves from the same tree. Each child chooses and examines one leaf then puts the leaf in a pile on the table. Leaves are gently stirred around and each child is challenged to find their leaf and explain how they know it is the right leaf.

Share this echo song.	*Children echo the leader.*
Leaves are turning,	Leaves are turning,
Turning brown.	Turning brown.
Watch the wind blow them	Watch the wind blow them
To the ground.	To the ground.

Marzollo, Jean. *I Spy Spectacular.* Photographs by Walter Wick. Scholastic, 2011. Ages 6–8.

Twenty years ago the author and photographer created the first book in this series, where children can spend hours hunting for hidden objects. Other books in the series include the following:

I Spy Spooky Night
I Spy School Days
I Spy Fantasy
I Spy Mystery
I Spy Fun House
I Spy Christmas
I Spy: A Book of Picture Riddles.

Mayhew, James. *Katie and the Sunflowers.* Orchard, 2001. Ages 5–7.

Madcap fun mixes with art history when Katie is so taken with Van Gogh's *Sunflowers* that she reaches into the painting to try to take some seeds. Sing the flower song (Tune: "Row, Row, Row Your Boat"):

> *Plant, plant, plant the seeds,*
> *Plant them in a row.*
> *Give them water, give them sun,*
> *Watch the flowers will grow.*

Napoli, Donna Jo. *Ready to Dream.* Illustrated by Bronwyn Bancroft, Bloomsbury, 2009. Ages 6–9.

On her trip to Australia, Ally discovers art can be created in many ways and using many different materials, not just paints and paper.

Activity: Create collages using things that are pleasing to touch, including materials which are rough, smooth, bright, dull, patterned, plain, large and small objects and things that make lines, such as string, yarn and ribbon, which can be moved in and out and around to make pathways for the design.

Peot, Margaret. *Inkblot, Drip, Splat and Squish Your Way to Creativity.* Boyds, Mills, 2011. Ages 10+.

Ten Tips for Looking at an Inkblot:

1. Look at the positive shapes — the ones made by ink and water.
2. Look at the white space around the images made by ink and water
3. What is the action like in the inkblot? Is it fast, splashy, slow, trickly?
4. Is this inkblot heavy or light, cloudlike or dense?

  5. Is this a secret picture or a billboard for everyone to see?
  6. Do you see two things side by side or one thing facing you?
  7. Where is this inkblot? In water? In the air? Underground?
  8. Is this inkblot loud or quiet?
  9. Is this inkblot hot or cold?
  10. Turn the inkblot upside down and try these questions again.

Raffin, Deborah. *Mitzi's World*. Illustrated by Jane Scott. Abrams, 2011. Ages 4–6.

  Follow the dog Mitzi through all four seasons as she explores towns and the countryside. Seek and discover more than 150 details in 15 works of folk art. Find candy canes in winter, sailboats in spring, sand castles in summer and pumpkins in fall.

  Art Activity: Create a hand turkey. Draw on a piece of paper around your hand. The thumb becomes the head, the fingers are the feathers. Color the turkey and mount on construction paper.

Rylant, Cynthia. *Brownie and Pearl See the Sights*. Illustrated by Brian Biggs. Beach Lane Books, 2011. Ages 3–5.

  Brownie and Pearl are off to see the sights. Join them as they bundle up and head outside to explore their neighborhood on a beautiful snowy day. They visit all their favorite spots, like the shoe shop and the hat shop, before discovering the city's sweetest sight of all. Cupcakes anyone?

  Do echo reading of the following poem:

On a cold winter day	On a cold winter day
We look up high	We look up high
To see big snowflakes	To see big snowflakes
In the sky.	In the sky.
Did you ever wonder	Did you ever wonder
What it takes	What it takes
For nature to make	For nature to make
Such big snowflakes?	Such big snowflakes?

Steiner, Joan. *Look Alikes: Seek and Search Puzzles*. Little, Brown, 2011. Ages 5–12.

  The more you look the more you see in Look Alike Land. In this book the reader will encounter not only look-alikes but puzzles, including find and match, brainteasers and more for visual/spatial thinkers. Introduce children to homophones, words that SOUND ALIKE but are spelled differently: (I began to BAWL when I was hit with a BALL, My AUNT gave me an ANT farm). Challenge children to make up sentences with these SOUND ALIKES: ate/eight, bare/bear, be/bee, blew/blue, cell/sell, chews/choose, close/clothes, doe/dough, flea/flee, made/maid

Thompson, Sarah L. *Imagine a Day*. Paintings by Rob Gonsalves. Atheneum, 2004. Ages 6–8.

An introduction to surrealism as the reader sees a sand castle on a high cliff taller than the children building it, along with of host of other things that don't belong in a realistic scene. The same author/illustrator in 2008 created a follow-up picture book, *Imagine a Place*.

Activity: Name the person, place or object that does not belong:

In the big city cars go by.
Tall buildings stretch and touch the sky.
Little Red Riding Hood walks right by.
(Red Riding Hood would not be walking in the city.)

Twelve little girls on a farm
Keeping Madeline safe from harm.
Ducks quack quack and hens cluck cluck
Wishing twelve little girls good luck.
(Madeline and the twelve little girls would not be on a farm.)

In the town be sure to stop
At the Night Kitchen Bakery Shop.
On the shelf there sits a toy
And its name is Corduroy.
(Corduroy does not belong in a bakery. He sits on a department store shelf.)

SEVEN

Developing Critical Thinking

What Is Critical Thinking?

Teaching critical thinking can begin in early childhood. Many picture books are problem solving experiences and can be used to teach the important thinking skills of decision-making and problem solving. In Pat McKissack's *Flossie and the Fox*, Flossie lives with Big Mama in the Piney Woods. One morning Big Mama asks Flossie to take a basket of eggs to Miss Viola, who lives on a farm on the other side of the woods. On the way Flossie meets the fox (who loves eggs).

Step one in problem solving is to define the problem. How can Flossie get through the woods safely and keep the fox from getting the eggs?

Step two is to list several ideas (or ways to solve the problem). Flossie could go back home and ask Big Mama to go through the woods with her. She could try outrunning the fox or she could keep the fox so busy that he will forget about the eggs.

Flossie chooses the latter action and fools the fox into believing that she doesn't know what kind of creature he is. Fox becomes more and more frustrated trying to convince Flossie that he is, indeed, a fox but to no avail — until the very last moment when she reaches the farm and he is chased off by a dog.

This kind of experience stimulates neural growth in both the upper and lower left brain quadrants — those that control verbal, analytical, sequential, logical thought. Note, however, that at one point in the

106

process the upper right quadrant was called into play — thinking of several possibilities for solving the problem. The lower right quadrant interacts when children state how they feel when Flossie, all alone in the woods, meets the fox.

Another enduring classic by Virginia Lee Burton presents several problems needing solutions. In *Mike Mulligan and His Steam Shovel* Mike finds that their services are no longer needed. Mike is jobless. After having children look at the pictures to gain an understanding of the job of a steam shovel, ask them, "Who might need Mike and Mary Ann to work for them?" Mike does get a new job, digging a cellar for the Town Hall, which he must do in one day in order to get paid. He accomplishes the task but discovers he had not given May Ann a way to escape from the hole. What will he do? Here again is practice in problem solving.

Critical Thinking and Academic Success

Much of the work of Paul Torrance shows little relationship between a student's academic success and job success. Many college graduates who passed tests by memorizing, retaining and giving back information were unable to solve problems or to think of new ideas on their own — skills highly valued by most employers.

The invasion of mediocrity into our lives and into our classrooms produces incalculable loss. The tyranny of modern thought sets limits on mental powers and obscures potential excellence. Good literature can lure it to the surface.

Creative Problem Solving

Sylvester and the Magic Pebble by William Steig. Aladdin Books, 1987.

Sylvester did not make a very good wish about what to do when he met the lion. What other action could he have taken that would have been better than his wish to become a stone? Score each action: 1=no, 2=maybe, 3=yes.

Action	Safe from lion	Can go home	Can keep pebble	Total
Stand still	1	1	3	5

Total the score for each wish. The best wish would be _____.

ANOTHER PROBLEM TO SOLVE

The Problem: In *The Little Old Woman and the Hungry Cat* by Nancy Polette a very greedy cat gobbles down sixteen cupcakes, a man and his pig, a wedding party and a little old woman and her sewing basket. With a snip, snap of her scissors the little old woman cuts a hole in the cat's side big enough to get through and they all step out to have a feast. The cat must spend the rest of the day sewing up the hole in its side. Suppose the old woman had forgotten her scissors. How else might she help everyone to get out of the cat? (The first is done for you.)

List your ideas	Fast	Safe	Effective	Total
Tickle the cat	3	2	3	8

A Critical Thinking Lesson

Horton Hatches the Egg by Dr. Seuss

In this tale of faithfulness and responsibility, Mayzie the lazy bird takes off for a vacation, leaving Horton the elephant to sit on her nest. Horton sits through the fall and through the ice and snow of winter, for "an elephant's faithful one hundred per cent." When spring comes, hunters capture Horton and sell him to a circus, tree, nest and all. While he is on display Mayzie happens to fly by. She stops to chat just as the egg begins to break apart. Now Mayzie wants to claim the offspring even though she did none of the work in hatching it.

1. Read the story aloud to the point where Mayzie the lazy bird returns to claim her egg.

2. Divide the group into those taking the part of Mayzie and those taking the part of Horton.

3. Ask each group to give five reasons why the egg should belong to their character. Reasons must be based on fact. Example: In nature elephants do not raise birds.

4. After each group has given its reasons let the class vote on who should get the egg: Horton or Mayzie? Share the ending of the story. Did the children like or dislike the way Dr. Seuss solved the problem?
5. Other questions to think about include these.

> Should wild animals be taken from their natural homes and put on display in circuses or zoos? Why or why not?
>
> Is it possible for an elephant to sit on an egg without breaking it? Why or why not?

BOOKS THAT ENCOURAGE CRITICAL THINKING

Note: While a few new titles have been selected for this section, the majority of the titles included here are classics of children's literature and should be found on most library shelves. Their enduring value makes them "must share" titles for young children.

Agee, John. *The Incredible Painting of Felix Clousseau.* Farrar, Straus & Giroux, 1988. Ages 4–8.

> Felix Clousseau, an unknown painter, enters a painting in a Paris exhibition which includes paintings by world famous artists. His painting of a duck is so lifelike (it quacks) that he wins the grand prize and people flock to buy his paintings. However, when his volcano painting erupts, the cannon painting explodes and the waterfall painting floods a house, the angry people have Felix put in jail. All of his paintings are confiscated except one. This one overlooked painting, of a watchdog, which hangs in the palace saves the day when a thief tries to steal the king's jewels. Here is an excellent title for evaluation. Should people embrace the new and different regardless of the consequences? Just because something is new or different does that make it better? Is progress always positive? Should Clousseau have been jailed for giving people what they wanted?

Barrett, Judi. *Cloudy with a Chance of Meatballs.* Illustrated by Ron Barrett. Aladdin Books, 1978. Ages 4–6.

> There were no supermarkets in the town of Chewandswallow, since breakfast, lunch and dinner fell from the sky. Breakfast began with a shower of orange juice followed by low clouds of sunny-side up eggs and toast. Lunch might be frankfurters already in their rolls followed

by mustard clouds. People listen to the weather report to find out what they will be eating the next day. It is quite a nice arrangement until one day the weather takes a turn for the worse. The food that falls from the sky gets larger and larger and so do the portions. The residents of Chewandswallow fear for their lives and have to escape. Ask: Is not having to work for food and shelter a good thing? How can the people of Chewandswallow escape? Where can they go?

Brett, Jan. *The Hat.* Putnam, 1997. Ages 4–6.

Suppose you had something on your head that made you look silly and everyone laughed as you walked by. That is exactly what happens to Hedgie the hedgehog when he walks past Lisa's clothesline and a sock gets stuck to his prickles. As each of his animal friends remark on the sock, Hedgie informs them that it is a hat to help him keep warm when the winter snows come. Lisa discovers her sock is missing and finds Hedgie. She retrieves the sock, telling him that "animals do not wear clothing." Ask: What do you think? Should the animals have made fun of Hedgie's hat? Should Lisa have let Hedgie keep her sock? Why or why not?

Bunting, Eve. *Fly Away Home.* Illustrated by Ronald Himler. Houghton Mifflin, 1991. Ages 6–8.

The only home Andrew and his dad have is the airport. "It's better than the streets," Dad says. "It's warm. It's safe. And the price is right." What Dad says is true. But still, Andrew hopes that one day life will be the way it used to be. Then he and his dad can have a place of their own again. The first rule for living in the airport is not to get noticed. Andrew and his Dad stay with the crowds and change airline waiting areas often. When Andrew sees a small trapped bird fluttering in the high hollow spaces he whispers for it to "fly away home." When the bird finally does escape, Andrew sees hope for himself and his Dad. Ask: Why do you think some people are homeless? What can be done to help homeless people?

Burton, Virginia Lee. *The Little House.* Houghton Mifflin, 1942. Ages 4–6.

The little house sits on a hill in the countryside and is happy watching the changing seasons and the activities she sees with each season.

The farmer plants and harvests his crops. In the summer the children swim in the pond and in the fall they go to school. She likes watching the children on their sleds in the winter and seeing the apple trees bloom in the spring. But roads are built, surveyors come and soon houses, then tall buildings and a whole city grow up around her. She misses the daisies and the apple trees and seeing the children at play. She is forgotten until one day a lady sees her. The lady had played in the house as a child. She buys the house and has it moved to the country, where once again the little house can watch the seasons come and go. Ask: Would you rather live in the city or the country? Why?

Cherry Lynne. *The Great Kapok Tree*. Harcourt Brace, 1990. Ages 5–8.

Tired from chopping the huge trunk of a tree, a young man becomes weary and sits down to rest under the great kapok tree. The creatures who live there are concerned, for they need the tree. The bee and the snake use the tree as a home. Others warn that destroying the trees will rob the land. The predators, concerned about their food supply, urge the man to consider carefully before cutting more trees. All who live there fear for the life of the rain forest. Suddenly, the young man wakes from his deep dream. The animals of the rain forest wait and wonder. Ask: Will the man leave the rain forest to grow and flourish? Will the animals live there in peace? What do you think the man should do? Why?

Clifford, Eth. *Flatfoot Fox and the Case of the Missing Eye*. Illustrated by Brian Lies. Houghton Mifflin, 1990. Ages 5–8.

Flatfoot Fox, the smartest detective in the world, is sitting in his office, just waiting for something to happen, when in walks Fat Cat. Fat Cat is mean and Fat Cat is mad — and what's more, Fat Cat has a mystery to be solved.

Detective Fox and his faithful assistant, Secretary Bird, set out to discover who has been the thief at Fat Cat's birthday party. Flatfoot Fox finds the culprit in true detective style, of course, but before the case is closed the two have met a zany assortment of suspects, starting with a Really Ridiculous Rabbit. Flatfoot Fox proves how clever he is. Ask: What facts that you find in the story help you solve the mystery?

Cronin, Doreen. *Click, Clack Moo: Cows That Type.* Illustrated by Betsy Lewin. Simon & Schuster, 2000.Ages 4–6.

Farmer Brown has a problem. His cows like to type. All day long he hears click, clack, click, clack moo. But Farmer Brown's problems really begin when his cows start leaving him notes. They demand electric blankets because the barn is cold at night. Not only do they demand the blankets, but they also refuse to give milk until they receive blankets.

Farmer Brown is furious and refuses to give the cows the blankets, so the cows go on strike and will not give milk. The hens, who are cold, too, join in the strike and refuse to lay eggs. Duck serves as the neutral party and takes notes back and forth between the farmer and the cows. Before finishing the story ask: Did farmer Brown take good care of his animals? Why or why not? Were the animals' demands reasonable? Why or why not?

Cronin, Doreen. *Duck for President.* Illustrated by Betsy Lewin. Simon & Schuster, 2004. Ages 4–8.

Farmer Brown and all of the animals have a lot of work to do to keep the farm running smoothly. One of Duck's jobs is to cut the grass. He does not like work of any kind and especially does not like cutting grass, since small blades of grass get caught in his feathers. Duck decides an election is needed to see who will run the farm. Duck campaigns, registers voters and wins the election. However, Duck finds that running a farm is hard work so he decides to run for governor instead. Again, he takes his message to the voters (a message only the duck voters can understand) and wins the election. However, Duck finds that being governor means lots of hard work. He decides to run for president. He gives speeches, appears on TV and wins the election. Duck does not find life in the Oval Office easy. It is hard work. Duck hates hard work. Ask: What do you think Duck will do now? Will Farmer Brown want Duck to return to his farm? Why or why not?

Egan, Tim. *The Trial of Cardigan Jones.* Houghton Mifflin, 2004. Ages 4–6.

Cardigan Jones, the moose, was seen walking by a window just as a pie was cooling on the ledge. The pie disappeared. Cardigan is put on trial, accused of stealing the pie. The jury thinks Cardigan is guilty even before all of the evidence is presented. Both Mrs. Brown and the milkman testify to seeing Cardigan by the window. During the trial, clumsy Cardigan knocks over statues and chairs and even upsets the judge. Before reading the outcome of the trial, ask the children: did Cardigan steal the pie? What evidence do you have in making your decision?

Estes, Eleanor. *The Hundred Dresses.* Illustrated by Louis Slobod-kin. Harcourt Brace, 1944. Ages 5–8.

Wanda wears the same faded blue dress to school every day. It is always clean but sometimes it looks as though it has been washed and never ironed. Peggy starts the game of the dresses when suddenly one day Wanda says, "I have a hundred dresses at home — all lined up in my closet." After that, it is fun to stop Wanda on the way to school and ask, "How many dresses did you say you have?" "A hundred," she answers. Then everyone laughs and Wanda's lips tighten as she walks off with one shoulder hunched up in a way none of the girls understand. Ask: How did the game Peggy and her friends played make you feel? How do you think the game made Wanda feel? What might you have done if you saw Peggy playing the game?

Forest, Heather. *Big Quiet House.* Illustrated By Susan Greenstein. August House, 2008. Ages 4–6.

"There once was a man whose house was very small," the story opens. "It was cluttered with things from wall to wall." With a tiny, cluttered house, giggling children, and a snoring wife, the poor man can't get a good night's sleep. If only, he thinks, I had a big quiet house! He throws off his covers and goes to visit the wise old woman at the edge of the village. Surely she can help him solve his problem. And she does, but not without giving him some very unusual advice. "Bring a chicken into your house," she suggests. And when that doesn't work, she has him add a goat, a horse, a cow, and a sheep. Ask: Why do you think the old woman has told the man to bring all of these animals into his house?

Fox, Mem. *Koala Lou.* Illustrated by Pamela Lofts. Harcourt Brace, 1989. Ages 4–6.

Koala Lou is the pride and joy of her parents. One hundred times a day her mother tells her how much she loves her. Then Koala Lou's brothers and sisters are born and mother is so busy looking after the little ones that she does not have time for Koala Lou. To get her mother's attention, Koala Lou decides to enter the Bush Olympics. She practices and practices to be ready for the big event. However, it is Koala Klaws who wins the tree climbing contest and Koala Lou is heartbroken. She returns to her spot in the blue gum tree late at night feeling very sad, until something happens to make her feel better. Ask: What do you think happens? Did Koala Lou have to win a contest for her mother to love her? Why or why not?

Garland, Michael. *Grandpa's Tractor*. Boyds Mill, 2011. Ages 5–8.

Once, the farmer's best friend was a red tractor. Back then, the pastures were filled with cows, and the fields were full of corn. Today, the cows are gone and the rows of corn have been replaced with row after row of identical houses. Grandpa Joe brings his grandson Timmy back to the site of the family farm, where the old house and ramshackle barn still stand. The shiny red tractor is now rusting in the forgotten fields. Ask: Which is needed more, houses or crops in the fields? Why do you think so? Are there cows and fields today? Where? What should be done to be sure we have both food and houses?

Gerstein, Mordicai. *The Man Who Walked Between Two Towers*. Roaring Brook Press, 2003. Ages 5–8.

In 1974 a young French aerialist has a dream. He loves to walk and dance on a rope tied between two trees, but his dream is to perform high in the air on a tightrope tied to the two towers of the almost completed World Trade Center in New York City. To do this, however, he will be breaking the law. Secretly he dresses as a construction worker in order to get his very heavy reel of cable and other equipment into the elevator. Working with a friend they then carry everything up 180 stairs to the roof. He shoots the line from one tower to the other with an arrow and then ties the cable on which he will walk. By dawn Philippe is ready for his walk. For more than an hour he walks and dances on the cable a quarter of a mile in the sky. After his performance, which startles many New Yorkers watching below, he is taken to jail and brought before a judge. Ask: What punishment do you think the judge will give the man for breaking the law?

Henkes, Kevin. *Chrysanthemum.* Greenwillow, 1991. Ages 4–7.

Because her parents thought she was an absolutely perfect baby they gave her a very special name, Chrysanthemum. Chrysanthemum loves her name, especially when mother uses it to wake her up or father uses it to call her to dinner. But going to school for the first time is a shock. The other children make fun of her name. They say it is too long and will not fit on her name tag. They say she is a flower to be picked and smelled. Each day Chrysanthemum takes longer and longer to get to school. When she is chosen to be a daisy in the school musicale the others laugh again. Before the children hear the satisfying ending to the story, ask: How would you feel if you were Chrysanthemum? Is it right to make fun of someone else? Why or why not?

Henkes, Kevin. *Lilly's Purple Plastic Purse.* Greenwillow, 1996. Ages 4–6.

Lilly loves everything about school, the pencils and chalk, her desk, the shiny hallways, school lunches and her teacher. At home she plays school with her brother, Julius. Yes, school is a wonderful place to be until the day she takes her new glittery glasses and purple plastic purse to school. She is so anxious to share her new things that she ignores her teacher's warning to wait and interrupts the class to show off her new things. When her teacher, Mr. Slinger, takes the things to keep for her until the end of the day, Lilly is furious. She draws a terrible picture of Mr. Slinger and adds terrible words to it and puts it into his book bag. At the end of the day Mr. Slinger gives Lilly her purse and glasses to take home. When she looks in her purse she finds a note from her teacher and what it says makes Lilly ashamed of what she has done. But it is too late to get the picture back. Ask: What do you think Lily should do?

Lester, Helen. *Batter Up Wombat.* Illustrated by Lynn Munsinger. Houghton Mifflin, 2006. Ages 5–8.

It's a brand new baseball season and the Champs are ready to go in their spiffy new uniforms. Never mind that the previous year they finished last in the North American Wildlife League, this season will be different. But when a wombat wanders onto the field on opening day, the Champs have no idea just how different the game is to become. Wombat has never played baseball. He is a very friendly fellow and wants to help out but he is puzzled over the terms. To Wombat, home plate is a dish, a bat is a furry creature, a pitcher is a container for milk and a foul is a chicken. When he is told to steal third base, he doesn't know where to hide it. It seems that Wombat does everything wrong until a large black cloud covers the field and Wombat saves the day. Ask: Should poor players be allowed to be part of a sports team? Why or why not?

Lionni, Leo. *Frederick*. Pantheon, 1967. Ages 4–6.

The mouse family is preparing for winter, gathering corn, nuts, wheat and straw. They work day and night to store enough food to last through the cold winter months. But Frederick does not gather food or straw. He gathers colors and words, which the other mice think are foolish things to gather. Then winter comes and when the cold seeps through the granary and the food supply is almost gone, Frederick shares his words and colors and the other mice find that these are fine things to store indeed. Ask: Would it have been better for Frederick to gather food for the coming winter rather than words and colors? Why or why not?

Pfister, Marcus. *Rainbow Fish*. North-South Books, 1995. Ages 4–6.

Rainbow Fish has no equal in the ocean for beauty. He is talked about and greatly admired by all the other sea creatures, for his scales sparkle and shine with many colors — purple, green, silver and blue. The more he is admired, the prouder he feels. Then comes a day when a very small blue fish asks Rainbow Fish for one of his scales. Of course, he refuses. The loss of even one scale might mar his extraordinary beauty. The blue fish is upset because Rainbow Fish will not share and he tells all the other ocean creatures. It isn't long before Rainbow Fish has no one to play with. Everyone ignores him. When he asks the octopus what he should do, the octopus tells him that unless he shares his scales he is doomed to a life of loneliness. Ask: Do you think Rainbow Fish will choose beauty or the companionship of the other ocean creatures?

Tarbescu, Edith. *The Boy Who Stuck Out His Tongue.* Illustrated by Judith C. Mills. Barefoot Books, 2000. Ages 5–7.

When the widow asks her son to light the fire, he just sticks his tongue out at her. "I'm too busy," he laughs, for he would rather make snowballs than help with chores. But when he gets himself into a sticky situation, the kind folk of the little Hungarian village are quick to rally around. The butcher, the baker, the cobbler, the carpenter and the cook gather up their tools and offer their well meaning support to the boy, but it is the blacksmith's hot coals that solve the problem.

Welling, Peter J. *Shawn O'Hisser: The Last Snake in Ireland.* Pelican Books, 2009. Ages 5–7.

In this fast-paced new twist on an old tale, whimsical snake Shawn O'Hisser returns to his native Ireland from a visit to England and Wales to find that all of his snake friends have vanished, as has all the leprechauns' gold. Shawn works to solve the mystery, using his wits to avoid being eaten by other inhabitants of the Emerald Isle. Things look pretty hopeless until Shawn is befriended by Edmund, the toad, and Kathleen, the orange mouse. Together, they set out to right a wrong, but will they solve the mystery in time? Ask: Will they find the leprechauns' gold, or did Dobherchu the Giant Otter take it? What did the monk named Patrick have to do with all those snakes disappearing?

Wood, Don and Audrey. *Heckedy Peg.* Harcourt Brace, 1987. Ages 5–8.

A mother has seven children named Monday, Tuesday, Wednesday, Thursday, Friday, Saturday and Sunday. She goes into town, promising to bring each child a gift if they will not let strangers into the house or play with fire. The children forget her warnings when Heckedy Peg offers them gold to let her in and light her pipe. She turns each child into a food, puts the food in her sack and takes them with her. When the mother, who arrives home, is told by a little bird what happened, she sets off to rescue her children. Before finishing the story, tell the children this: The only way she can do this is to guess which food each child has become. Do you think she can do it? Can you?

Wood, Don and Audrey. *King Bidgood's in the Bathtub.* Harcourt Brace, 1985. Ages 3–6.

King Bidgood likes his bathtub. In fact, he likes it so much that he refuses to get out of it. All day long a young page cries for help from the court to get the king out of the tub. The queen suggests lunch. "We will lunch in the tub," roars the king. A knight calls the king to battle. A duke suggests fishing. The entire court invites the king to a party but none of these ideas work. Night comes and the king is still in the tub. At last the page has an idea. Ask: How do you think the page will get the king out of the tub?

Wood, Don and Audrey. *The Little Mouse, the Red Ripe Strawberry and the Big Hungry Bear.* Scholastic, 1994. Ages 3–6.

A little mouse finds a huge red, ripe strawberry and gets a ladder to climb up to pick it. Then Little Mouse is told about the hungry bear that loves red, ripe strawberries. Bear will tromp through the forest following the smell of a ripe strawberry that has just been picked. Moue tries hiding the strawberry and putting a chain around it. Mouse tries disguising the strawberry as a person. The mouse discovers there is only one way to keep a hungry bear from getting the strawberry. Ask: Can you think of a way mouse can keep thee hungry bear from eating all of the big, ripe strawberry?

Yorinks, Arthur. *Hey, Al.* Illustrated by Richard Egielski. Farrar, Straus & Giroux, 1986. Ages 5–7.

Al, a poor janitor, lives in one room with his dog, Eddie. Eddie is tired of being poor and longs for a better life. He gets his wish when Al is visited by a large bird who promises to take Al and Eddie to a place where they can have everything they desire and where there is no work. At first Al and Eddie enjoy the beautiful place where they can eat and drink and swim whenever they wish. Then one day Al discovers that their noses are beginning to look like beaks — they are slowly turning into birds. As the two escape, Al believes that Eddie has drowned in the ocean and is very sad. But the two are eventually reunited and discover that friendship is the best gift of all. Ask the children to imagine that everyone decided not to go to work. What would happen?

EIGHT

Developing Positive Relationships and a Positive Self-Image

The Affective Domain

Of all of the thinking abilities necessary for a satisfying and productive life, none is more important than those that touch the affective domain — the development of a positive self-image and the ability to interact successfully with others. These are the interpersonal and intrapersonal skills, which include the ability to relate to and understand others and one's self, to see other points of view and to sense the feelings of others. Using both verbal and nonverbal means of communication, children with well-developed interpersonal and intrapersonal skills work well in groups. They are also self-aware and clear about their own feelings and emotions.

In experiences over the years as director of the Laboratory School at Lindenwood University, this author has met many concerned parents who want only the best for their child — intellectually. These parents are not only overly concerned with skill and drill, from flash cards to computer drills, but they also feed their children a steady diet of fact books, from astronomy to geology. These truly caring parents need to be helped to understand that their children need books to touch their heart and to help their humanity keep pace with the growth of intellect. Exposure to fine literature can help the heart to sing along with the mind!

Literature and the Needs of Young Children

The following books address some of these needs.

THE NEED TO KNOW

McDonald, Megan. *Is This a House for Hermit Crab?* Help Hermit Crab find a new house and escape the pricklepine fish!

THE NEED TO ACCEPT AND GIVE LOVE

Hest, Amy. *The Dog Who Belonged to No One.* A little lost dog and a lonely little girl find each other.

THE NEED TO ACHIEVE AND FEEL SELF ESTEEM

Lovell, Patty. *Stand Tall, Molly Lou Mellon.* Molly Lou is short and clumsy with a bullfrog voice, but she doesn't mind, as she takes her grandmother's advice to heart, especially when a bully picks on her.

THE NEED FOR BEAUTY, ORDER AND HARMONY

Priest, Robert. *The Pirate's Eye.* The world becomes a beautiful place when seen through the eyes of another.

THE NEED TO COPE WITH STRESS

Williams, Linda. *Little Old Lady Who Was Not Afraid of Anything.* All of the scary things the old lady meets on her way home turn out to be just what she needed!

THE NEED TO BELONG

Probably the most famous book ever written about finding one's place in the world is Hans Christian Andersen's *Ugly Duckling.* Every human being will be rejected by someone at some time. Every child, too, is a priceless being and must come to believe in their self worth. Is the *Ugly Duckling* a simple story? Yes, it is simple but it is a strong lesson in humanity.

The Power of Literature

It is often helpful to lure children to a realistic, problem-solving story. The child should be given time to think about the problem and to suggest more than one idea for solving the problem. For example, in Eve Bunting's *Fly Away Home* what child cannot help but be touched to discover that the only home Andrew and his dad have is the airport. "It's better than the streets," Dad says. "It's warm. It's safe. And the price is right." What Dad says is true. But still, Andrew hopes that one day life will be the way it used to be. Then he and his dad can have a place of their own again. The first rule for living in the airport is not to get noticed. Andrew and his Dad stay with the crowds and change airline waiting areas often. When Andrew sees a small trapped bird fluttering in the high hollow spaces he whispers for it to "fly away home." When the bird finally does escape, Andrew sees hope for himself and his Dad. Stories like *Fly Away Home* can be very effective in helping children walk in another's shoes and wrestle with problems that are not easy to solve.

Yesterday's bright children of technology have taken us outward to the moon, but have we traveled far enough to find our own hearts? Yesterday's young intellectuals have built nuclear power plants, but have we found the power which reinforces all life? Yesterday's quiz kids have built bridges which span the waters between nations but have we bridged the chasms of prejudice and bigotry among and within nations?

Children's books abound with themes dealing with life's stresses and losses. Exposure to these books can help the child identify with a character and experience the same wide range of emotions the character experiences as life's losses are confronted. Every good story contains conflict. Through literature, as children experience the ways in which others meet and deal with adversity, compassion and feelings begin to develop.

Consider for a moment the bill parents eventually pay for using television rather than literature to capture the child's attention. Watch the typical Saturday morning cartoons. What is the level of language used? Simple or complex? How are the problems solved? Through violence or through reasoned dialogue? How much time is the child given to observe a visual before it is replaced by another? Could there be a connection between the rapid changes of visuals and subjects on television and the growing number of primary teachers reporting children with attention deficit disorder? What real human feeling is the child getting from the television cartoon? Is the bill too high?

QUESTIONS THAT ENCOURAGE INTERPERSONAL THINKING

One of the ways to encourage affective thinking is to ask children questions like those below:

1. What is your favorite story? Why is it your favorite?

2. Has the artist of the picture book given each character colors that show feelings? What colors give you different feelings?

3. Which was your least favorite character in the story? Why?

4. Describe how the character (name) _____ felt when _____.

5. Pick your favorite character. If you could give that character a gift, what would the gift be? Why?

6. Think of the book character you would most like to be and tell why you would choose to be that character.

7. Think of two or three things you can say about yourself. Then name a story character who is the opposite of each thing you named.

8. Did you agree with the way the story problem was solved? Could it have been solved in a better way?

9. Work with a team of four to respond to a read-aloud story. Each team member will have a different task:

A Storyteller: In two or three sentences tell what the story was about.

B Word Collector: Name three or four colorful words you heard in the story.

C Connector: How is this story like another story you know?

D Artist: Draw a picture of your favorite part of the story.

10. Create report cards for two or more story characters. What grade would each receive in:

Graded for	Grade	Why
Generous	_____	_____
Kind	_____	_____
Responsible	_____	_____
Truthful	_____	_____
Honest	_____	_____
Courteous	_____	_____
Cooperative	_____	_____
Trustworthy	_____	_____
Friendly	_____	_____

The list of books that touch the heart is long and it would be impossible to compile a list that all would agree were the best of the best. The titles that follow are among this author's favorites and are representative of those gems of the past and newer titles that publishers hope will appeal to today's children. In searching for other titles to touch the heart that are appropriate for a specific child will find the help of the school librarian or the children's librarian at the public library can be invaluable.

BOOKS, QUESTIONS AND ACTIVITIES FOR AFFECTIVE THINKING

Allen, Elanna, *Itsy Mitsy Runs Away*. Atheneum, 2011. Ages 3–6.

Itsy Mitsy has had quite enough of bedtime. So tonight she's running away to the perfect place, where there are no more bedtimes ever (not even one). But running away isn't as easy as it seems. There's a lot to pack: Mitsy's friendliest dinosaur, Mister Roar; a snack for Mister Roar; Mitsy's dog, Pupcake (to keep the bedtime beasties away from said snack)— the list goes on and on. But with a helpful dad who makes sure Mitsy doesn't leave anything behind, especially not him, Mitsy might want to run away tomorrow night, too.

Ask: What do you suppose will happen to Mitsy if she runs away at night all alone? Is running away from bedtime a good idea? Why or why not?

Balouch, Kristen. *The Little Girl with the Big Big Voice*. Little Simon Books, 2011. Ages 3–5.

There once was a little, little girl with a big, big voice. One day she goes out to find someone to play with. She searches the jungle high and low but her big voice scares all of the animals away. One by one an elephant, a snake and a croc quickly retreat from the girl's booming vocals, until at last she finds the perfect playmate, who is even louder that her big, big voice. Ask: Who do you suppose her new playmate is?

Collect books with different wild animals on the cover. Ask children to make noises like the animals. Create a "Loud Poem." Finish these lines:

> Being loud doesn't matter. Hear the monkeys _____(chatter).
> Take a peek. Hear the little mouse _____ (squeak).
> Make that sound some more. Hear the lions _____(roar).
> Hear the gray wolves howl. Hear the tigers _____ (growl).

Bardoe. Cheryl. *The Ugly Duckling Dinosaur*. Illustrated by Doug Kennedy. Abrams, 2011. Ages 5–8.

Once upon a time, seven tiny duck beaks pecked their way out of their eggs, but the eighth egg is a little bit different. What emerged isn't a duck at all. He is a dinosaur! Everyone notices how different he is. He doesn't waddle. His teeth are too big. Feeling ugly and outcast, the dinosaur duckling leaves his family and ventures out on his own. Again and again he tries to make friends but everyone runs away. Over time he grows bigger and bigger but still can't seem to find his rightful place. Unexpectedly he comes across other dinosaurs that look just like him and discoverers he's really a T-Rex. Ask: How many ways is this story like Hans Christian Andersen's *Ugly Duckling*? How is it like *Cinderella*?

Play the Animal Game. Show one child a picture of an animal and have him whisper a description to the next child. After several children have passed on the description, ask the last child to describe the animal to the others. Can they guess what the animal is?

Bates, Jane. *Seaside Dream*. Illustrated by Lambert Davis. Lee & Low, 2011. Ages 4–6.

Tomorrow is Grandma's birthday, and the house is overflowing with family and friends. Cora is excited but she is also worried because she still does not have a present for Grandma. Cora cannot think of anything special enough. Cora knows her grandmother misses her home country, Cape Verde. After a nighttime walk on the beach with Grandma, Cora finally comes up with an idea for the perfect gift. It is one that both of them will always remember and a way to help Grandma reconnect with a faraway family.

Ask: What might this perfect gift be? Do you think it is something Cora will buy at the store? Why or why not? Draw a picture of something you would see if you took a nighttime walk with a grandparent around your neighborhood.

Bunting, Eve. *Tweak, Tweak.* Illustrated by Sergio Ruzzier. Houghton Mifflin, 2011. Ages 3–5.

Little Elephant and Mama Elephant are going for a walk. "Hold on to my tail," says Mama. "If you want to ask me a question, tweak twice."

Tweak! Tweak! "Mama, what is that?" Little Elephant is curious about the frog, the monkey, the songbird, the butterfly and the crocodile and especially about what a little elephant can do. Mama knows just how to answer to help her cherished little elephant grow. Complete these sentences:

Little elephant and his mama walk in the _____.
I walk in the _____.
Little Elephant asks his mama, _____?
I ask my mama, _____?

Carlstrom, Nancy. *It's Your First Day of School, Annie Claire.* Illustrated by Margie Moore. Abrams 2011. Ages 4–6.

It's Annie Claire's first day of school and she doesn't know what to expect. What if she snores during nap time? What if the other kids count and color better than she can? What if no one plays with her? Here is a gentle tale that will calm fears and excitement for the special new school year ahead. Ask: Suppose a new student arrived for a first day in your class. Name five things you could do to make the child feel welcome.

Play Pack a School Lunch. Children sit in a circle. The leader says, "In my lunchbox I will put an apple." Another child adds a food to the lunchbox that begins with B. The game continues as the children name foods from A to Z (skip X) until 25 foods have been named.

Dunrea, Oliver. *Appearing Tonight! Mary, Heather, Elizabeth Livingstone.* Farrar, Straus & Giroux, 2000. Ages 5–8.

Mary Heather is a star by the age of three, appearing nightly onstage to sing and recite. She longs for an ordinary life and eats and eats until she literally outgrows stardom. Eventually, a world that ejects her because of her appearance learns to accept her as a person with unique gifts.

Activity: Every child has a talent. Identify the talent of each child in the group and have each child draw a self portrait and label his talent. Talents might include these: kind, organized, brave, good worker, neat, artist, singer, good listener and many others.

Freedman, Claire. *Where's Your Smile, Crocodile?* Illustrated By Sean Julian. Peachtree Publishers, 2010. Ages 4–6.

Kyle the crocodile wakes up feeling grumpy. All his friends do their best to cheer him up, but it's only when Kyle meets a lost lion cub that he discovers that helping someone else is a great way to find your smile. Ask the children to suppose their best friend was feeling sad or grumpy and name five ways to cheer them up.

Glass, Beth Raisner. *Blue Ribbon Dad.* Illustrated by Margie Moore. Abrams, 2011. Ages 4–6.

A little boy thinks of all the special things he does with his dad — schoolwork, reading, swimming lessons, haircuts and more. He decides to craft a present, a homemade blue ribbon, to show his dad how much he loves him. The boy counts down the hours until his dad comes home, recalling their favorite memories and preparing the special gift.

Activity: Make a blue ribbon gift for someone who is special to you. Cut out describing words from newspaper ads and staple them to the ribbon. Words that appear in many advertisements include: GREAT, TERRIFIC, THE BEST, THE ONE AND ONLY, SUPER, and many others.

Holmes, Janet A. *Have You Seen Duck?* Illustrated by Jonathan Bentley. Cartwheel, 2011. Ages 3–5.

A young boy and his soft plush pal are inseparable. But when Duck goes missing, the boy is inconsolable and goes in search of his friend. "He won't know what to do without me," he says. The boy asks the shopkeeper, the postman, the bus driver and the dog next door. No one has seen duck. Back at home, what is hiding between the couch cushions? Duck! Ask: If Duck had not been found, would another toy do just as well to make the boy happy? Why or why not?

Suppose the child rode a bus around town looking for his duck. Add words to the "Wheel on the Bus" song. Sing to "Here We Go Round the Mulberry Bush."

The wheels on the bus go round and round, round and round, round and round.
The wheels on the bus go round and round, Early in the morning.
The wipers on the bus go _____, _____, _____.
_____, _____, _____. _____, _____,
_____.
The wipers on the bus go _____, _____, _____,
early in the morning.

Encourage children to add other verses with the last verse being:

The ducks on the bus go quack, quack, quack, quack, quack, quack, quack, quack, quack,
The ducks on the bus go quack, quack, quack, early in the morning.

Kaplan, Bruce Eric. *Monsters Eat Whiny Children.* Simon & Schuster, 2011. Ages 5–8.

Dad has warned Henry and Eve: If you whine too much, monsters will hear you. Henry and Eve don't listen, of course. The only problem is, when the monster comes he can't find the right recipe for whiny children, and neither can his monster friends. A whiny child salad doesn't work because there's paprika in the dressing. A whiny child cake won't do because the flour spills all over the floor. And whiny child burgers are out of the question because the grill is too hard to light up. And just when the monsters decide on the perfect dish the worst thing of all happens. Ask: What do you suppose it is?

Show books of recipes. Ask the children to create a recipe for a drink that would cure children from whining. Use the quantities in one of the recipes in the book but ask children to change the ingredients.

Mix: 2 cups of _____ with 2 cups of _____.

Add ½ cup of _____ and a tablespoon of _____.

Stir in 3 cups of _____ and beat for _____ minutes.

Pour into a large pot _____.

McDonnell, Christina. *Goyangi Means Cat.* Illustrated by Steve Johnson and Lou Fancher. Viking, 2011. Ages 4–7.

When Soo Min comes from Korea to live with her new American family, she struggles to learn English and adjust to unfamiliar surroundings. She finds great comfort in the family's cat, Goyangi — that is, until he runs away. After searching the streets, Soo Min discovers her beloved pet has returned to the house, and she speaks her first English words, "Goyangi home."

Ask the children to suppose they met a child from another country who did not speak English. Ask: How could you let that child know you want to be their friend?

Create a Cat Joke Book. Think of words that rhyme with cat: bat, brat, chat, fat, flat, hat, mat.

Ask a question: What do you call a cat that misbehaves? A brat cat.

Numeroff, Laura. *Would I Trade My Parents?* Illustrated by James Bernardin. Abrams, 2011. Ages 5–8.

What child hasn't thought about trading their parents for the ones next door? Who wouldn't be discouraged if their parents didn't allow them to have pets or go camping or drink chocolate milk before dinner? A little boy ponders why his friend's parents are so special and why sometimes he wishes he could trade. But then he remembers his very own parents and all the amazing things that only they know how to do, like the way they always read with him and leave notes in his lunchbox or take him on family bike rides. In fact, his parents are the best of all. Ask the children to list five ways their parents or grandparents help them and list five ways the child can help them. Ask the children to ask their parents, grandparents or caregiver at home to name something we use today that was not available when they were six or seven years old. Ask each child to draw a picture of the item. Put together a class book titled: "Mother [or Dad or Grandma or Grandpa] Didn't Have These."

Parr, Todd. *I'm Not Scared Book.* Little, Brown, 2011. Ages 3–5.

Sometimes I'm scared of dogs.
I'm not scared when they give me kisses.
Sometimes I'm scared I will make a mistake.
I'm not scared when I know I tried my best.

Everyone is afraid sometimes but most of the time we don't need to be afraid. Finish these sentence starters:

I'm not scared of storms when _____.
I'm not scared of dark houses when _____.
I'm not scared of wild animals when _____.

Polette, Keith. *Moon Over the Mountain* Illustrated by Michael Kress-Russick. Raven Tree Press, 2008. Ages 5–10.

Told in English and Spanish, here is the tale of the lonely stonecutter who is unhappy with his lot in life. The Great Spirit grants his wishes to become a wealthy merchant, the sun, the wind and finally the mountain. It is just as he feels he is the strongest thing on Earth that the chisel of a stonecutter cuts into his side. Share Gerald McDermott's story of *The Stonecutter.* Find the similarities in the stories.

Activity: Create a machine. Just as the Stonecutter disliked his job of chipping away the mountain each day, we all have chores we don't enjoy. Draw or construct a machine that will do a chore for you. You can use paper, boxes, plastic bottles or cans. When your machine is ready to be viewed you should be able to answer three questions: What does it look like? What does it do? How does it work?

Raschka, Chris. *Little Black Crow.* Atheneum, 2011. Ages 4–6.

A little boy wonders about a crow's life, from the simple — "Where do you go in the cold, white snow?" — to the not-so-simple — "Do you ever worry when you hop and you hurry?" Ask: "Are you ever afraid of mistakes you made? Are you never afraid?"

Play Change Places. Line up the children in the front of the room.

One child is seated and calls out: "Robin, change places with crow." The children holding the robin and crow cards try to change places before the seated child reaches the vacant space. The child left standing calls out two other birds. Give each child a card with the name and/or picture of a different bird.

Rayner, Catherine. *The Bear Who Shared*. Dial, 2011. Ages 4–6.

Norris the bear has been waiting patiently for the last ripe fruit to fall from the tree. But Tulip the raccoon and Violet the mouse have, too, although not quite so patiently. In fact, Tulip and Violet sniff, listen to, and even hug the fruit. Norris catches the fruit when it finally falls, and because he is a wise bear, he shares it and makes two new friends.

Play the fruit game. Place the name of each fruit on a different card: apple, pear, orange, plum, banana, cherry, lemon, lime, melon. Each child gets a different card. One child comes to the chalkboard or chart and draws a line for each letter in the fruit he has (example ___ ___ ___ ___ ___ ___ [orange]). Another child guesses a letter and tells on which line the letter should go. If correct, he can continue guessing letters until a guess is incorrect. Then another child takes a turn. The game continues until the fruit is guessed.

Ryan, Pam Munoz. *Tony Baloney*. Illustrated by Edwin Fothering-ham. Scholastic, 2011. Ages 4–6.

As the only boy sandwiched between two many sisters, Tony Baloney seems doomed to a life of trouble. Most of the time when he is tired of playing with Bossy Big Sister Baloney (who always makes him be the kitty) and exasperated with the Bothersome Babies Baloney (who drool on his toys), his very best stuffed animal buddy, Dandelion, behaves badly. And then, Tony must say he is sorry, which is not always easy.

Activity: Ask children to tell about the good things of being part of a family (of having brothers and sisters). Hand out strips that say: "If it weren't for you _____." Ask each child to think of one person who has done something for them and write to that person by finishing the sentence. (Sentences can be dictated for children not yet reading or writing.) Each child gives his sentence to the person. If not a family member a classmate could be chosen.

Schachner, Judy. *Skippyjon Jones, Class Action.* Dutton, 2011. Ages 4–6.

Skippyjon Jones really wants to go to school. School is for dogs, his mama tells him. It's where they go to get trained. But nothing can stop Skippy. Once inside his closet he finds himself on the playground of his imagination, surrounded by dogs of all kinds. He bays with the beagles, learns French with the poodles, and checks out a Chihuahua book from the library. And when a bully starts sending shiver-itos down the spines of the little yippers, Skippy saves the day and earns the biggest gold star.

Activity: Talk about the importance of working together. Compose a group poem (it does not have to rhyme) about working together, with each child calling out lines as you write them down. Then read all the lines together as one poem.

Sheridan, Sara. *I'm Me!* Illustrated by Margaret Chamberlain. Chicken House, 2011. Ages 3–5.

Grown-ups! Always telling kids what to do, how to act, who to be! Imogen is happy to spend the day with Auntie Sara, but which dress-up game doe she want to play? Who is Imogen today? Is she a frilly princess in a poofy gown? A knight in shining armor, taming a flying dragon? An astronaut blasting off into space? "No, no, no," Imogen sings, with a shake of her head and a smile on her face. Auntie Sara asks, "Then who do you want to be?" "I'm me!" Imogen declares. Because being herself is the most fun of all.

Complete the poem using a princess, a knight or an astronaut.

> I wish I were (what?) An airplane pilot.
> Doing what? Flying a jet.
> Where? High in the sky.
> Why? Taking people where they want to go.

Smith, Cynthia Leitich. *Holler Loudly.* Illustrated by Barry Gott. Dutton, 2010. Ages 4–7.

Holler Loudly has a voice as big as the Southwestern sky and everywhere he goes people tell him to "hush!" From math class to the movies and even the state fair, Holler's loud voice just keeps getting on people's nerves. But Holler can't help himself, being loud is who he is. Will Holler ever find a way to let loose his voice without getting into trouble?

Share: Create a group poem about loud things. It does not have to rhyme. Ask each child to dictate one line beginning with "Louder than." The last line will read, "That's how Holler Loudly sounds." Read all the lines together as a single poem.

Tillman, Nancy. *Tumford the Terrible*. Fiewel and Friends, 2011. Ages 3–5.

Tumford isn't really a terrible cat. He just has a way of finding mischief—tracking dirt into the house, knocking over breakable things, and disrupting fancy parties. But even though he feels bad, he has a hard time saying, "I'm sorry." Will the fact that his owners love him, no matter what, help Tumford say the magic words?

Activity: A simple shape for a cat can be made by folding a piece of construction paper in half and cutting a half circle from the middle. Mount on construction paper and add a head and tail with crayons or markers. Give the cat a name. What is one thing your cat might do that it has to say "I'm sorry!" for? Share *Cookie's Week* by Cindy Ward. Compare Cookie and Tumford.

Yee, Wong Herbert. *Mouse and Mole: A Winter Wonderland*. Houghton Mifflin, 2011. Ages 4–6.

Yippee! It's snowing like mad! It is a winter wonderland. What better day for Mouse and Mole to go sledding, whirl around on ice skates and build snowmen together? But Mole doesn't want to go outside, Too cold! Too windy! He prefers to stay as snug as a bug in a rug inside his nice warm bed. Mouse is lonely. Ice skating and sledding just aren't as much fun for one. Then she gets an idea—a Sno-Mole might do the trick. Mole won't be needing his hat or scarf or mittens. Or will he?

Activity: Think of other ways that Mouse might get Mole out of bed using: a pan of water, a feather, a book, popcorn, ice cubes, a fan. Remember, Mouse wants Mole to be his friend.

NINE

The Natural World

The Naturalistic Thinker

People with high naturalistic intelligence, whether adults or children, are very aware of their place in nature and highly attuned to the outside world. Time spent outdoors is much preferred to indoor activities. The naturalistic thinker is environmentally conscious. They are very alert on nature walks, noticing small aspects of the natural world that most others miss. The goal is protecting the natural world that we all share, perhaps by building habitats, planting and maintaining a garden, maintaining bird feeders or feeding wild animals when snow covers the ground.

Appropriate activities for naturalistic thinkers include the following:

• Nature walks in all kinds of environments.
• Collecting objects from nature for a collage.
• Building animal shelters, including bird houses and deer feeders.
• Grouping and classifying plants, animals, rocks, minerals and other objects found in nature, for example, grouping wildlife by location:

1. African Grasslands	4. Himalayas
2. Arctic Ocean	5. Australia
3. Desert	6. Turtle Islands

_____ elephants _____ snow leopards _____ whales
_____ herons _____ camels _____ crabs

_____ cobras   _____ polar bears   _____ yaks
_____ dingoes   _____ koala bears   _____ lions

• Observing, locating and naming the stars and constellations.
• Preparing projects that show understanding of the food chain.
• Preparing projects that show understanding of the water cycle.
• Becoming aware of environmental issues.
• Writing a book: "Saving the Planet A–Z." Each letter of the alphabet lists something a child can do to make our planet safer and healthier.

Sharing Informational Books on the Natural World

Informational books are rare treasures. The best are written with knowledge and enthusiasm and are beautifully and accurately illustrated. Nonfiction books today are a far cry from those of years ago. With improvement in color art technology and with the goal of authors to be entertaining as well as factual, today's books are a treat for the eye and mind alike.

Note the delicacy and grace and near poetic quality of these non fiction books by Diane Siebert as she takes children on a tour of deserts, prairies and mountains. Open the pages of *Mojave* to watch tumbleweeds bounce and roll along the ground. Lizards dart, tortoises creep, and snakes glide out of sight. The Mojave Desert is a special place. Its landscape is powerful and mesmerizing, with deep arroyos, the windstorm's sting of sand and dust, the cry of the bold, black raven above ghost towns that lie with crumbling walls, and the night songs of coyotes singing, "We are the desert, we are free."

In *Heartland* visit the midsection of America, "a place where golden wheat waves in the breeze, where great rivers flow, and cornfields stretch across the plains in glorious patchwork quilts of greens, yellows and browns. Cattle graze in lush green pastures, horses and sheep fill the barns, and a newborn calf stands damp and warm in the sun. This is the Heartland where the farmer is king, but over everything, Nature reigns supreme." In *Sierra* a giant rocky mountain speaks of beauty, life and endurance through the ages. It speaks for its tall sister peaks in the Sierra Nevada chain of mountains in California. They have survived glaciers and earthquakes. They support giant, centuries-old sequoia trees. Predators such as bears and mountain lions hunt the wildlife the mountains nurture. Now the peaks stand as sentinels watching as the ultimate predator, man, threatens all they protect and nurture.

Children will listen in fascination as these nonfiction books by Siebert are read aloud. These and many other of the best books on the outdoor world attempt to answer questions as well as leave the reader wanting to know more.

It is sometimes difficult to distinguish fiction from nonfiction books for very young children. Who can imagine an orangutan and a dog being friends? Is it even possible? With Suryia, the orangutan and Roscoe, the stray dog, it is! Set on a preserve for wild animals, *Suryia and Roscoe* is the true story of a remarkable, continuing friendship. The reader not only gains information about both animals but is also left with questions to think about. Will the two always be friends? What if another animal wanted to be friends with one or the other? What other animals are cared for on a wildlife preserve? Leaving the reader or listener with questions is a major goal of today's nonfiction writers.

Environmental Issues for Young Thinkers

In a country that is rapidly destroying its natural beauty, what better books to share with children than those that develop an appreciation for nature and the environment? Books like Ann Turner's *Heron Street* have great appeal to these children. She describes the long-ago marsh teeming with wildlife, herons, ducks, geese raccoons, rattlesnakes and wolves. But then men and women and children came and everything began to change. The people built houses and churches and made roads through the marsh. Slowly, as time passed and there was more building up and tearing down, the animals began to leave in search of wilder lands to live in. Here is a tale of progress and the losses it has caused in nature.

Two gifted author/illustrators used their skills more than 40 years ago to make a plea for protecting the environment. Both used fictional tales to deal with serious subjects. In Dr. Seuss' book *The Lorax*, a visitor arrives in a barren land and finds only an old "Once-ler" living there. It seems that many years before, the land was filled with beautiful Truffula trees, clear ponds, clean clouds and happy animals. Then one by one the trees were cut down to make products for people. A Lorax visited the Once-lers who were destroying the trees and warned them that all of the animals would disappear. The Once-lers ignored the warning until the last tree was cut down. The air was filled with factory smoke. The ponds were full of glump. The birds and animals were gone. With a sad face the Lorax takes leave of the polluted land, leaving a small pile of rocks with just one word: UNLESS!

The Wump World, created by Bill Peet, shows the Wumps living in a world of grassy meadows and leafy green trees surrounded by winding rivers and lakes. It is a happy, pleasant world until one day a great flock of potbellied monsters land in the meadow and belch forth pollutions with their giant machines. The Wumps tumble down into a dark cavern as the machines gobble trees and grind them to bits. The Pollutions were constructing their "wonderful new world." Meanwhile, the Wumps remained underground, frightened by the endless noises. Would the Wumps ever see their beautiful world again?

Can progress be stopped? Should it be stopped? Can humans live in harmony with nature without destroying the planet they inhabit? These are weighty questions for the young naturalistic thinker to ponder. After sharing *The Lorax* with older children and *The Wump World* with younger children, share some of the nonfiction titles that show what the young naturalistic thinker can do to help the natural world.

In Loreen Leedy's *A Great Trash Bash,* the mayor of Beaston can't figure out what is wrong with the town until one day he slips on a banana peel and realizes the town has too much trash. A town meeting is called and all the citizens put their heads together to solve the problem. They decide that incinerators burn trash and create energy but cause air pollution. Trash dumped in the ocean pollutes the water. The only answer is to change the way they live. They learn to buy products in returnable containers, to return food scraps to soil in compost bins, and to reuse rather than to buy new things. The citizens of Beaston learn to be real trash bashers!

Going Green: A Kid's Handbook to Saving the Planet by John Elkington teaches the young environmentalist about the three Rs—REUSE and RECYCLE as much as possible, and REFUSE to buy environmentally unsafe products — and how to conduct a green audit of home, school and community, and suggests projects children can do to solve environmental problems.

BOOKS AND ACTIVITIES TO USE
TO EXPLORE THE NATURAL WORLD

Informational books abound on every aspect of the natural world. Steve Jenkins' *Living Color* combines easy-to-understand language with colorful illustrations of the animal world. Diana Aston's *A Butterfly Is Patient* is a gorgeous and informative introduction to the world of butterflies. *Desert Elephants*, with bold and dramatic illustrations by Helen Cowcher, captures the beauty, harmony and wisdom of these great beasts. The list of beautiful books to share goes on and on.

A visit to the children's section of he library will boggle the mind with additional endless choices. Whatever book a parent or teacher chooses to share that is sourced in the real world is providing an experience that is enhanced by all of the books shared previously. We could liken the consciousness of each child to a giant jigsaw puzzle, with pieces missing here and there. Each literary experience can perhaps fit a missing piece of the puzzle into the whole, until a worldview is achieved which is solid and beautiful.

The newer titles presented at the end of this chapter are by no means meant to be first choices in sharing informational books on the natural world with children. The field is vast and the titles included here are meant to be representative of the vast treasure storehouse awaiting parents, grandparents, teachers and children in the library.

Aston, Dianna Hutts. *A Butterfly Is Patient*. Illustrated by Sylvia Long. Chronicle Books, 2011. Ages 4–6.

From iridescent blue swallowtails to brilliant orange monarchs to the world's tiniest butterfly (Western Pygmy Blue) and the largest (Queen Alexandra's Birdwing), an incredible variety of butterflies are shown here in all their beauty and wonder. Sing the following to "I'm a Little Teapot":

Look at the butterfly
That grew from a caterpillar,
Slowly, slowly from a caterpillar.
In the chrysalis it grew and grew.
Look at the butterfly, it's looking at you!

Balas, Vincent, and Lucie Durbiano. *Where Is Your Home?* Houghton Mifflin, 2011. Ages 2–4.

A friendly dog and cat help a small frog search for the perfect home. The little reader can slide the sturdy tabs to reveal an owl in his nest, a fox in her den, a monkey in a cage. Will dog and cat find the perfect home for little frog? Keep sliding and see.

Activity: Tell the children that most frogs live in ponds. Other creatures also live in ponds. Assign "noisy" parts that the children will say when you point to them. Beavers say "Chew, chew, chew." Owls nod, nod, nod. Tadpoles wiggle, wiggle, wiggle. Bees buzz, buzz, buzz. Frogs hop, hop, hop, Snakes slither, slither slither.

POND LIFE

Life Around the Pond

Brown beavers
Chew, chew, chew.
Wise old owls
Nod, nod, nod.
Silver tadpoles
Wiggle, wiggle, wiggle,
Busy as can be.

Yellow bees
Buzz, buzz, buzz.
Four fat frogs
Hop, hop, hop.
Two black snakes
Slither, slither, slither.
Look around and see
Having fun
In the sun.
Life around the pond.

Brown, Marc. *Arthur Turns Green.* Little, Brown, 2011. Ages 4–6.
Arthur is full of ideas when it comes to doing his part to save the planet. But is he actually turning green? Arthur comes home from school and sneaks around the house, taking notes and talking about a Big Green Machine. D.W. is suspicious of her brother's weird behavior, and when Arthur shows up late for dinner with green hands, she really gets the creeps! Will the Big Green Machine get her, too? Activity: What ideas can children add to save the planet?

    If I were in charge of keeping the world clean
    I would _____
    and _____
    because _____.
    But the most important thing I would do to keep the world
    clean would be _____.

Carle, Eric. *The Very Hungry Caterpillar.* Philomel Books, 1969. Ages 3–5.
Imagine how exciting it would be to travel on an adventuresome journey into the life of a caterpillar. It certainly would be interesting to experience all the changes a caterpillar goes through from the time it is hatched from an egg and spins a cocoon until it emerges as a beautiful butterfly. On a beautiful, sunny Sunday morning a little egg does hatch and out comes a green, fuzzy caterpillar. This caterpillar is very hungry so he eats everything he can find, including cake and pickles. In fact, the caterpillar eats so much that he gets a stomachache. But before he can spin his cocoon he has to eat something else. Can you guess what it is?

    While the raindrops fell a little _____ hid in a
    _____. The rain stopped and out came the
    _____.
    On Monday it _____.
    On Tuesday it _____.
    On Wednesday it _____.
    On Thursday and Friday it _____.
    On Saturday it was so _____ that it
    _____ and _____ and it
    decided to _____ on Sunday.

Castillo, Lauren. *Melvin and the Boy.* Henry Holt, 2011. Ages 4–7.

When a little boy sees a turtle basking in the sun, he thinks he's found the perfect pet. But when they get home, the boy soon discovers that the only time the turtle comes out of its shell is at bath time. Is it possible that the turtle will be happiest back at the pond? After all, it's always bath time there.

Sing the Turtle Song to the tune of "Did You Ever See a Lassie?"

> *Did you ever see a turtle, a turtle, a turtle,*
> *Did you ever see a turtle,*
> *Take a bath in a pond?*

Other last lines can be: "Peek out of his shell" and "Hide in the grass." Add other lines the children suggest.

Cooney, Barbara. *Miss Rumphius.* Viking, 1982. Ages 5–8.

Miss Rumphius' first name is Alice and when she was small she dreamed of traveling to faraway places and living by the sea. Her grandfather told her that she must also make the world a more beautiful place in which to live.

Miss Rumphius *did* travel to faraway places and saw coconuts and cockatoos on tropical islands, lions in the grasslands and monkeys in the jungle. On a hillside she found lupine and jasmine growing and rode a camel across the desert to meet a kangaroo in an Australian town. Yes, Miss Rumphius did almost everything she wanted to do. In her later years she even lived by the sea. But what can she do to make the world a more beautiful place? What ideas do you have for Miss Rumphius to make the world more beautiful?

Activity: Give a verbal flower to a friend. The flower must begin with the same letter as the friend's first name, for example, John gave a tulip to Tina.

Cowcher, Helen. *Desert Elephants.* Farrar, Straus & Giroux, 2011. Ages 4–8.

Each year the desert elephants of Mali, West Africa, travel a 300-mile path to search for water. They peacefully pass through the lands of the Tuareg, Dogon and Fulani people while following the longest migration route of any elephant in the world. Discover how people work together to preserve the delicate balance of life in the desert and protect these magnificent elephants. Share this poem:

> Out on the desert in the noonday sun
> Lived a mom and papa elephant
> And their little calf one.
> "Follow us," said the mother.
> "I follow," said the one
> As they walked and they walked in the noonday sun.

Cowcher, Helen. *The Rain Forest*. Farrar, Straus and Giroux, 1988. Ages 5–7.

Many animals, plants and insects live in the rain forest. Among them are sloths, tapirs, jaguars, macaws and monkeys. They live in harmony until the day when man with his powerful machine comes to cut down the trees. The animals' fear causes them to seek high ground. Then the floods come forth. With no trees to hold the soil in place, the swirling water washes away man and his machine. Although the animals are safe on high ground as the story ends, we wonder, as they do, how long the tall trees will be there to protect them.

Activity: Pretend you have stepped into the rain forest. Complete the following lines about your experience.

Into the tropical rain forest
  Over _____
  Under _____
  Above _____
  Between _____
  Lives a _____.

Cronin, Doreen. *Diary of a Worm*. Illustrated by Harry Bliss. HarperCollins, 2003. Ages 5–7.

A little worm learns about life and records his daily experiences in diary form. The reader meets his family and learns important rules for life from mother worm: (1) The earth gives us everything we need, (2) When we dig tunnels we help take care of the earth, (3) Never bother daddy when he's eating the newspaper.

Meet worm's friend spider and discover the dangers of fishing season and hopscotch. Laugh with worm as he scares three little girls. Learn about the importance of good manners and what happens if a worm eats before it goes to bed. Like children, worm has his likes and dislikes. He would like to grow up to be a secret service agent and protect the president. He dislikes homework and is unhappy that he can't chew gum or have a dog. Yet he notes that worms never have to go to the dentist or take a bath, and tracking mud through the house is okay.

Activity: List things worm did in the story:

dug tunnels
taught spider

_____

_____

_____

_____

Put two of the things you listed on the lines in the song below. Sing to the tune of "London Bridge."

Example: *Wiggly worm dug tunnels,*
Dug tunnels,
Dug tunnels.
Wiggly worm dug tunnels
And taught spider.

Cyrus, Kurt. *Big Rig Bugs*. Walker, 2011. Ages 4–8.

Lifting, sorting, digging and hauling are dirty jobs, so when a construction worker throws away a half-eaten sandwich, a crew of bugs gets to work clearing the area of debris. An ant works like a forklift, a cricket acts like a bulldozer. Readers will be fascinated to see how each bug has a unique way of getting the job done. Ask children to complete the pattern:

We see bugs —
(color)_____ bugs, (color) _____bugs.
We see bugs (where?)_____.
We see bugs (doing what?)_____.
Bugs in a rug, bugs in a jug,
Bugs climbing up a red fireplug!
We see bugs!

Cyrus, Kurt. *The Voyage of Turtle Rex*. Houghton Mifflin, 2011. Ages 5–8.

Sploosh! Fizz! Swish! The prehistoric ocean is a dangerous place for a baby sea turtle. But after she emerges from her egg, the treacherous waters are her goal. Swimming through the swirling waves and dodging larger sea creatures, she finds a resting place deep below. There she waits, until she grows into the majestic sea turtle that returns to the sand to lay her own eggs and begin the cycle again.

Activity: Show several books with pictures of sea creatures on the cover. In small groups or as partners ask the children to pick a sea creature and complete the pattern:

> I see a (sea turtle) and the (sea turtle) sees me
> It was (swimming) along in the deep blue sea.
> (Sea turtle) goes (Sploosh! Fizz! Swish!)

Galbraith, Kathryn. *Planting the Wild Garden*. Illustrated by Wendy Halpeerin. Peachtree, 2011. Ages 4–8.

A farmer and her son carefully plant seeds in their garden. In the wild garden, many seeds are planted, too, but not by farmer's hands. Different kinds of animals transport all sorts of seeds, often without knowing it. Sometimes rain washes seeds away to a new and unexpected location. And sometimes something extraordinary occurs, as when the pods of Scotch broom burst open explosively in the summer heat, scattering seeds everywhere like popcorn.

Activity: Take a nature walk with the child/ren in a field or woods. Give each child a small bag. Look for things to collect, such as twigs, leaves, pods, a feather, seeds. Glue the items on colored construction paper for a nature collage.

Gourley, Robbin. *First Garden: The White House Garden and How It Grew*. Clarion Books, 2011. Ages 6–8.

The White House kitchen garden was started by First Lady Michelle Obama to encourage healthful eating. This is the story of that garden as well as the story of other gardens on the White House grounds, including Eleanor Roosevelt's victory garden in World War II. It tells of the teamwork involving local children as well as the Obama family and the White House staff that led to the garden now flourishing on the South Lawn.

Activity: The growth of a lima bean can allow children to view the rooting process firsthand. Give each child one lima bean, one dampened paper towel, one plastic bag and tape. Put the bean on a towel, place it in the bag, and tape to their desks. They can witness the miracle of growth on their own.

Henkes, Kevin. *Kitten's First Full Moon*. Greenwillow, 2004.

It is evening and kitten has taken a stroll from the porch of the home where she lives. Suddenly she sees the moon. Kitten is sure that it must be a bowl of milk in the sky. Perhaps if she opened her mouth wide, the milk would fall from the sky. Unfortunately the only thing that falls from the sky is a bug. Kitten tries reaching the milk from the top of the tallest tree. When kitten looks down from the tree to the pond she sees another bowl of milk. She jumps down from the tree and leaps into the pond. The bowl of milk disappears and kitten crawls out wet and still hungry. As the unhappy kitten once again reaches the porch of her home, what does she find there but a bowl of milk.

Activity: Read each statement and ask the child/ren to guess yes or no. Then share the poem that has the answers.

1. ____ A newborn kitten does not have teeth.
2. ____ Cats have rough tongues.
3. ____ The paws of a cat are hard.
4. ____ There are five claws on each paw.
5. ____ Cats communicate with each other with their whiskers.
6. ____ Cats catch and eat mice.

ABOUT CATS

A new-born cat has teeth to bite,
The rough-tongued cat sees well at night.
They reach out soft paws,
On each is five claws.
With whiskers they talk,
As dinner they stalk,
And big cats give small mice a fright.

James, Simon, *Dear Mr. Blueberry*. Margaret McElderry Books, 1999. Ages 4–7.

It is vacation time, so Emily has to write to her teacher for help: "Dear Mr. Blueberry, I love whales very much and I think I saw one in my pond today. Please send me information about whales." Mr. Blueberry answers at once, pointing out that whales live in salt water, not in ponds, so it can't be a whale. But Emily believes in her whale and replies that she is putting salt into the pond every day before breakfast and that she has seen the whale smile. After several letters Mr. Blueberry explains more forcibly that a whale cannot live in Emily's pond, they are migratory, meaning they swim long distances each day, they do not get lost and they eat shrimplike creatures. Emily then reports that her whale has then become migratory again and has left the pond. She is sad. But in her last letter she has a happy surprise to tell Mr. Blueberry and all is well.

Share Mother Goose rhymes related to the ocean: "Row, Row, Row to Georgia Bay," "Bobby Shaftoe's Gone to Sea," "Rub-a-Dub Dub, Three Men in a Tub." Explain that a map is a picture of places in the world. Show on a map where whales can be found in the world. Collect books with cover illustrations of other ocean creatures. Ask the child/ren to arrange the books from the largest to the smallest ocean creature.

Jenkins, Steve. *Living Color*. Houghton Mifflin, 2011. Ages 4–6.

Here is a whole world of colorful animals, from the blue-tongued skink to the pink flamingo, with reasons for each animal's bright color, from attracting a mate to camouflage. Encourage children to draw and cut out their own colorful animal. Draw trees as a background on a large sheet of poster paper and attach the children's animals to the scene for a mural.

Krupinski, Laura. *Snow Dog's Journey*. Dutton, 2011. Ages 4–6.

On a frosty cold winter day, two children set out to build a snow dog. They find two shiny pebbles for his eyes and one for his nose. To keep him warm, they wrap a scarf around his neck. Then one night the Frost King breathes magic into the dog. Though he's made of snow and ice, the snow dog can now run and play, and he goes off on a great adventure with the Frost King. But he never forgets the children who love him, and one day he decides to find his way back to them. Explain the difference between fact and fantasy. Ask: What parts of this story could be fact? What parts of the story are fantasy?

Show children a copy of *The Farmer's Almanac*. Explain that it tells what the weather will be. Compare the daily forecast with the forecast in the paper for three days. Make a chart:

Date	Farmers Almanac	Local Paper	Actual Weather
(1) _____	_____	_____	_____
(2) _____	_____	_____	_____
(3) _____	_____	_____	_____

Lyon, George Ella. *All the Water in the World*. Illustrated by Katherine Tillotson. Atheneum, 2011. Ages 6–8.

We are all connected by water. Where does water come from? Where does water go? Find out in this exploration of oceans and waterways that highlights an important reality. Our water supply is limited, and it is up to us to protect it. Ask children to respond to the following statement: Suppose all the rivers dried up. Where might wild animals find water?

Write a river song! Use names of creatures that make the river their home. Sing to the tune of "The Bear Went Over the Mountain."

Example:

We saw a trout in the river,
We saw a trout in the river,
We saw a trout the river,
For the river is its home.
We saw a _____ in the river,
We saw a _____ on the river,
We saw a _____ by the river,
For the river is their home.

Martin, Jacqueline Briggs. *Snowflake Bentley*. Illustrated by Mary Azarian. Houghton Mifflin, 1998.

Snow in Vermont is as common as dirt. Why would anyone want to photograph it? But from the time he was a small boy, Wilson Bentley thinks of the icy crystals as small miracles and he determines that one day his camera will capture for others their extraordinary beauty. Often misunderstood in his time, Wilson Bentley took pictures that even today reveal two important truths about snowflakes: first, that no two are alike, and second, that each one is startlingly beautiful. Here is the story of a simple farmer who not only had a scientist's vision and perseverance, but also a clear passion for the wonders of nature.

Before reading *Snowflake Bentley* find out what members of your class have in common with the characters and setting of the book. Ask: Who???

1. Likes winter as the best of all seasons?
2. Likes to play in the snow?
3. Can make a paper snowflake?
4. Has lived on a farm?
5. Has taken a picture with a camera?

Newman, Mark. *Polar Bears.* Henry Holt, 2011. Ages 4–6.

Whose fur isn't really white? Who usually gives birth to twins? Who's the biggest bear in the world? The polar bear! Full of fascinating information, this book explores the world of the polar bear on land and underwater, from the baby cubs to the majestic adult bears.

Activity: Gather books on arctic animals to display. Allow children time to look through the books and choose an animal they would like to be. Allow the children to pantomime their animals for others to guess.

Perlman, Willa. *Good Night, World.* Illustrated by Carolyn Fisher. Beach Lane Books, 2011. Ages 3–5.

"Good night, sun and other stars. Good night, Saturn, Venus, Mars. Elsewhere in the world it's light. It's morning there, but here it's night." As the sun sets from east to west the reader is taken on a magical journey to bid good night to the world's natural wonders, from plants and animals to mountains, oceans and wide desert plains.

Activity: Before hearing the poem, match the animals below with their natural habitats. Guess if you do not know.

1. mountain   _____ lion
2. desert   _____ crab
3. jungle   _____ eagle
4. ocean   _____ coyote

The lion roars in its jungle home.
In the mountains eagles soar.
Coyotes howl at the desert moon.
Crabs crawl on the ocean floor.

Preus, Margi. *Celebritrees: Historic and Famous Trees of the World.* Illustrated by Rebecca Gibbon. Henry Holt, 2011. Ages 6–9.

Some trees have lived many years, standing as silent witnesses to history. Some are remarkable for their age and others for their usefulness. A bristlecone pine tree in California is more than 4,000 years old, and a major oak in England was used as a hiding place for Robin Hood and his men. These fourteen fascinating trees remind us not only of how much pleasure trees bring but also of what they tell us about history.

Activity: Take the child/ren on a nature walk where trees are growing. Ask them to observe as carefully as they can the trees they see. Do they see birds, nests, insects, broken limbs, moss? Which trees look young and healthy? Which trees look older? How do they know?

Sidman, Joyce. *Dark Emperor and Other Poems of the Night.* Illustrated by Rick Allen. Houghton Mifflin, 2011. Ages 6–8.

Welcome to the night, when mice stir and furry moths flutter. When snails spiral into shells as orb spider circle in silk. When the roots of oak trees recover and repair from their time in the light. When the porcupette eats delicacies, raspberry leaves, and coos to its mother. Come out to the cool night woods, and buzz and hoot and howl. But beware, for it's wild and windy way out in the woods.

Activity: To explore opposites, ask children to complete the following sentences by adding the missing word (words used are night, wake, dark, far, bright, down):

1. We play during the day but we sleep at _____.
2. During the day it is light. At night it is _____.
3. My night light is near but the moon is _____.
4. Light from a half moon is dull but light from the sun is

   _____.
5. I look up at the sky but I look _____ at the ground.
6. At night I sleep but in the morning I _____.

Sidman, Joyce. *Swirl by Swirl: Spirals in Nature.* Illustrated by Beth Krommes. Houghton Mifflin, 2011. Ages 6–8.

What makes the tiny snail shell so beautiful? Why does that shape occur in nature over and over again — in rushing rivers, in a flower bud, even inside your ear? Here is a look at many spirals in nature, from fiddleheads to elephant tusks, from crushing waves to spiraling galaxies.

Activity: Go on a nature walk. What shapes do children see? Give the child/ren a variety of cut-out shapes: squares, rectangles, triangles, hexagons, circles. Encourage them to create their own creatures from nature using any of the shapes they wish and adding to their creatures with crayons or markers.

Tresselt, Alvin. *White Snow, Bright Snow.* Illustrated by Roger Duvoison. Lothrop, 1947. Caldecott Winner. Ages 3–6.

The postman, the farmer, the policeman, the children and even the rabbits know it is going to snow. And sure enough from the low, grey sky the snowflakes come first one, then two, then a whole sky full. By evening the whole town is covered with the snowflakes that the children had tried to catch on their tongues. By morning automobiles look like "big fat raisins buried in snowdrifts." The postman puts on his high boots, the farmer milks his cows, the policeman stays in bed with a chill and the children make a snowman. As the days pass the snow disappears and signs of spring emerged, from small flowers to sunshine to the first call of a robin.

Sing the Story: Choose words from the box to complete each line in the song (tune: "Twinkle, Twinkle Little Star"):

ground	day	found	play	snowflakes

Children looking in the sky
Saw the (1)s_____ watched them fly.
Rabbits burrowed in the (2) g_____.
In the barn the cows were (3) f_____.
Then when night turned into (4) d_____.
Children all went out to (5) p_____.

Van Allsburg, Chris. *Just a Dream*. Houghton Mifflin, 2011.

Walter is a litterbug who does not appreciate the beauty of nature or understand his role in keeping the planet healthy — until a fantastic journey shows him the tragic fate that could befall Earth if humans like him are not more careful. Are Walter's actions really helping his planet along the road to destruction, or is it all just a dream? Complete the poem below that tells what we can do to take responsibility for the environment:

If we were in charge of keeping the world clean
We would _____
and _____ because _____.
But the most important thing we would do to keep the world
clean would be _____
If we were in charge of keeping the world clean.

Yezerski, Thomas F. *Meadowlands*. Farrar, Straus & Giroux, 2011. Ages 5–8.

The 20,000 acres of wetlands in New Jersey now known as the Meadowlands were once home to hundreds of species of plants and animals. But over hundreds of years people have dammed up, drained, built over and polluted this formerly vibrant ecosystem and all but destroyed it. Still, signs of life remain — under bridges, on the edges of parking lots, and beside train tracks. Slowly but surely, with help from activist groups, government organizations and ordinary people, the creatures of the Meadowlands are making a comeback, and the wetlands are recovering.

Complete this pattern for one of the wild creatures found in this book:

In the _____
By the _____
Between _____
Lives a _____ named _____.

Yolen, Jane. *Owl Moon*. Illustrated by John Schoenherr. Philomel, 1987. Ages 4–6.

A little girl is excited when her father takes her into the woods on a snowy night to see the Great Horned Owl. The two quietly make their way among the tall trees, calling to the owl. To their delight the owl answers.

Activity: As the Great Gray Owl watched above the forest he saw many forest animals. Here is a way to tell about the things he saw. Add more forest animals to this pattern:

Gray Owl. Gray Owl what do you see?
I see a red squirrel climbing for me.
Red squirrel, red squirrel what do you see?
I see a gray fox hiding from me.
Gray fox, gray fox what do you see?
I see a _____ looking at me.

Yolen, Jane. *Welcome to the Greenhouse* Illustrated by Laura Regan. G.P. Putnam's Sons, 1993. Ages 6–8.

Here is the mysterious world of the tropical rain forest, a house where giant forest trees form the walls and vines frame the views and there is no roof overhead, only a canopy of leaves. Everywhere, color threads through the hot greenhouse. By day you can hear exotic noises, the rustling of the green-coated sloth, or the chatter of monkeys as they make their way from room to room. A flash of the hummingbird or the silver streak of a lizard catch the eye and the ear picks up the crunch of the wild pig as it bites into tropical fruit. Listen carefully for the wings of the heron flapping to take off in flight, the swoop of the bat as it glides by the sleeping ocelot. Hear the prowling panther searching for its dinner.

> Welcome to the greenhouse.
> Welcome to the hot house.
> Welcome to the land of the warm, wet days.

Activity: Pretend you have stepped into the rain forest. Complete the following lines about your experience:

Into the tropical rain forest
Over _____
Under _____
Above _____
Between _____
Lives a _____.

Appendix:
Nancy's Choices —
Nonfiction Too Good to Miss!

Language Arts

Agee, John. *Elvis Lives and Other Anagrams.* Farrar, 2000 Ages 6–10. The author creates new words and phrases by jumbling the letters.

Goldstone, Bruce. *100 Ways to Celebrate 100 Days.* Holt, 2010. Ages 5–7. 100 ideas for celebrating the 100th day of school.

Henson, Heather. *That Book Woman.* Illustrated by David Small. Atheneum, 2009. Ages 6–8. The true account of the librarians who used pack horses and served the mountain people in the 1930s.

Joosse, Barbara. *Please Is a Good Word to Say.* Illustrated by Jennifer Pleecas. Philomel, 2007. Ages 4–6. A humorous approach to manners and phrases like "please," "excuse me" and "thank you."

Koontz, Dean. *Every Day's a Holiday.* Illustrated by Phil Parks. HarperCollins, 2003. Ages 4–8. Here are poems for every holiday, including unusual holidays like Praise-the-Chicken Day and Lost-Tooth Day.

Leedy, Loreen. *Crazy Like a Fox: A Simile Story.* Holiday House, 2008. Ages 6–9. A fun introduction to similes.

Leedy, Loreen, and Pat Street. *There's a Frog in My Throat.* Holiday House, 2003. Ages 5–10. 440 animal sayings, with an index to help readers find their favorites.

Linz, Kathi. *Chickens May Not Cross the Road and Other Crazy (But True) Laws.* Illustrated by Tony Griego. Houghton Mifflin, 2002. Ages 5–7. A collection of absurd laws that are still on the books, humorously illustrated in this volume.

Moses, Will. *Raining Cats and Dogs*. Philomel, 2008. Ages 6–8. A collection of idioms and illustrations.

Rylant, Cynthia. *The Beautiful Stories of Life*. Illustrated by Carson Ellis. Harcourt, 2009. Ages 6–8. Six Greek myths retold.

Singer, Marilyn. *Mirror, Mirror*. Dutton, 2010. Ages 6–12. Fairy tales as reversible poetry. Reads the same top to bottom or bottom to top, Highly recommended.

Truss, Lynne. *Twenty-Odd Ducks*. Illustrated by Bonnie Timmons. G.P. Putnam's Sons. Ages 5–7. Putting a punctuation mark in the wrong place can completely change the meaning!

Poetry

Ada, Alma Flor. *Pio Peep!* HarperCollins, 2003. Ages 4–8. Traditional Spanish nursery rhymes told in Spanish and English.

Chorao, Kay. *Rhymes Around the World*. Ages 4–8. Old favorites and new poems from England to Africa, Japan to Mexico and every corner in between. Delightfully illustrated.

Florian, Douglas. *Dinothesaurus*. Atheneum, 2009. Ages 4–8. Prehistoric poems and paintings ... all about dinosaurs.

Greenberg, David. *Don't Forget Your Etiquette*. Illustrated by Nadine Westcott. Farrar, 2006. Ages 5–7. The "essential guide to misbehavior" told in verse.

Harris, Jay M. *The Moon Is La Luna*. Illustrated by Matthew Cordell. Houghton Mifflin, 2007. Ages 4–8. Silly rhymes in English and Spanish.

Hopkins, Lee Bennett. *City I Love*. Abrams, 2009. Grades 1–4. 18 poems that lead the reader on a tour of the world's largest cities.

Hopkins, Lee Bennett, ed. *Oh No, Where Are My Pants?* Illustrated by Wolf Erlbruch. HarperCollins, 2005. Ages 6–9. Fourteen poems about disaster days — worm-in-the-apple days, friends-moving-away days and even forgetting-my-pants days.

Hughes, Ted. *Collected Poems for Children*. Illustrated by Raymond Briggs. Farrar, 2007. Ages 7–10. Over 250 poems for children that Ted Hughes wrote throughout his life.

Katz, Bobbie. *More Pocket Poems*. Illustrated by Deborah Zemke. Dutton, 2009. Ages 3–6. Short kid-friendly poems for every season. Most are eight lines or less.

Kuskin, Karla. *Moon, Have You Met My Mother?* Illustrated by Sergio Ruzzier. HarperCollins, 2003. Ages 5–8. The collected poems of Karla Kuskin.

Lewis, J. Patrick. *Please Bury Me in the Library*. Illustrated by Kyle M. Stone. Harcourt, 2005. Ages 6–8. Delightful poems about books and libraries, beautifully illustrated. A must have!

Lewis, J. Patrick. *A World of Wonders*. Dial, 2002. Ages 7–12. Geographic travels in verse and rhyme.

Low, Alice. *The Fastest Game on Two Feet*. Illustrated by John O'Brien. Holiday House, 2009. Ages 7–12. The history of many sports told in poetry.

Mak, Kam. *My Chinatown: One Year in Poems*. HarperCollins, 2002. Ages 5–7. Visit Chinatown, a place of dreams, fireflies, dragons and magic. Moving poems share a year of growing up in this small city within a city.

Mora, Pat. *A Pinata in a Pine Tree*. Illustrated by Magaly Morales. Clarion, 2009. Ages 4–6. Latino twelve days of Christmas.

Park, Linda Sue. *Tap Dancing on the Roof*. Illustrated by Istvan Banyai. Clarion Books, 2007. Ages 7–10. Three line SIJO poems from Korea with a twist in the third line.

Prelutsky, Jack, ed. *The Beauty of the Beast*. Illustrated by Meilo So. Knopf, 2006. Ages 5–8. Poems from the animal kingdom, with lyrical watercolor paintings.

Prelutsky, Jack. *The Frog Wore Red Suspenders*. Illustrated by Petra Mathers. Harper Trophy, 2005. Ages 4–8. Twenty-eight rhymes with colorful illustrations from the popular poet.

Prelutsky, Jack. *Read a Rhyme, Write a Rhyme*. Illustrated by Meilo So. Knopf, 2005. Ages 6–8. Rhymes chosen by a favorite poet with hints and starters for writing rhymes.

Prince, April. *Twenty-One Elephants* Illustrated by Francois Rcoa. Houghton Mifflin, 2003. Ages 6–8. Free verse tells of the building of the Brooklyn Bridge and the testing of its strength by P.T. Barnum's circus elephants.

Rose, Deborah Lee. *Into the A, B, C*. Scholastic, 2000. Ages 4–8. A colorful, rhyming ABC book that introduces a variety of ocean creatures.

Ruddell, Deborah. *A Whiff of Pine and a Hint of Skunk*. Illustrated by Joan Rankin. Margaret K. McElderry Books, 2009. Ages 4–8. Through the four seasons with animals of the forest. Fun poetry.

Schertle, Alice. *Wrinkled Rhymes*. Illustrated by Petra Mathers. Harcourt, 2009. Ages 4–8. A collection of poems about clothing.

Siebert, Diane. *Tour America*. Illustrated by Stephen Johnson. Chronicle Books, 2006. Ages 6–8. Familiar American landmarks described in lyrical verse.

Stevenson, James. *Corn Chowder*. Greenwillow, 2003. Ages 4–8. Illustrated poems about everyday things.

Music and Art

Aliki. *Ah, Music!* HarperCollins, 2003. Ages 5–7. An introduction to instruments, artists and performers.

Berkes, Marianne. *Over in the Ocean.* Illustrated by Jeanette Canyon. Dawn, 2004. Ages 5–7. Marine life introduced with music, math and colorful art.

Brenner, Barbara. *The Boy Who Loved to Draw, Benjamin West.* Illustrated by Olivier Dunrea. Houghton Mifflin, 1999. Ages 6–8. As a child Benjamin got in trouble for drawing instead of doing his chores. Finally, realizing that their son could not be "cured" of his drawing habits, Benjamin's parents arranged for art lessons. This boy who loved to draw became one of America's most famous artists.

Chambers, Veronica. *Celia Cruz: Queen of Salsa.* Illustrated by Julie Maren. Dial, 2005. Ages 6–8. A lively picture book biography of the singer who rose from humble beginnings to worldwide fame.

Cowling, Douglas. *Hallelujah Handel.* Illustrated by Jason Walker. Ages 5–8. Fictionalized biography telling how Handel donated proceeds from the Messiah to help poor and orphaned children.

Cunxin, Li. *Dancing to Freedom.* Illustrated by Anne Spudvilas. Walker, 2008. Ages 6–10. The true story of Mao's last dancer, a poor Chinese boy who danced in cities around the world.

George-Warren, Holly. *Honky Tonk Heroes and Hillbilly Angels.* Illustrated by Laura Levine. Houghton Mifflin, 2006. Ages 7–10. Short illustrated biographies of the pioneers of western music.

Gerstein, Mordicai. *What Charlie Heard.* Farrar, 2000. Ages 7–10. Charlie wanted to re-create all of the sounds that he heard in his childhood. He wrote music but others heard his music only as noise. The story of Charles Ives, the composer who persisted despite criticism of his music.

Hopkinson, Deborah. *Home on the Range.* Illustrated by S.D. Schindler. G.P. Putnam's Sons, 2009. Ages 6–8. The story of John A. Lomax and his cowboy songs.

Kimmel, Eric. *A Horn for Louis.* Illustrated by James Bernadin. Random House, 2006. Ages 6–8. An easy-to-read story of Louis Armstrong and his love affair with a horn.

Lach, William. *Baby Animals.* Metropolitan Museum of Art. Abrams, 2008. Ages 3–6. Simple text and paintings of baby animals from the Metropolitan Museum of Art.

Raffin, Deborah, *Mitzi's World.* Illustrated by Jane Wooster. Abrams, 2009. Ages 5–7. A seek and find book through all four seasons in cities and the countryside.

Ray, Deborah Kogan. *Wanda Gag: The Girl Who Loved to Draw.* Viking, 2008. Ages 5–7. The author/artist of *Millions of Cats* put aside her dreams of becoming an artist to steer her family through tough times. When the job was done she won scholarships to art schools, becoming a beloved children's author/artist.

Rodriguez, Rachel. *Through Georgia's Eyes.* Illustrated by Julie Paschkis. Henry Holt, 2006. Ages 6–8. The story of artist Georgia O'Keefe, who saw the world differently from most people and captured her visions in her paintings.

Schaefer, Carole Lexa. *Two Scarlet Songbirds.* Illustrated by Elizabeth Rosen. Knopf, 2001. Ages 6–8. When composer Anton Dvorak spent a summer in Iowa he was fascinated by the sounds of nature. Two songbirds in particular caught his interest and he tried to repeat their sounds in his music, which resulted in *The American Quartet*, a string quartet in F major.

Schulte, Jessica. *Can You Find It Inside? Can You Find It Outside?* Metropolitan Museum of Art/Abrams, 2005. Ages 4–6. The reader is asked to find objects in famous paintings. A creative introduction to the world of art.

Sturges, Philemon. *The Twelve Days of Christmas.* Illustrated by Ashley Wolff. Little, Brown, 2007. Ages 4–6. A lively Hispanic adaptation of a familiar Christmas song, "A Pinata for the Pinion Tree."

Warhola, James. *Uncle Andy's Cats.* G.P. Putnam's Sons, 2009. Ages 5–8. True story of the cats that played in Andy Warhol's art studio.

Wellington, Monica. *Squeaking of Art: The Mice Go to the Museum.* Dutton, 2000 Ages 5–8. An introduction to museums led by ten mice pals. Paintings are grouped by subject and are identified by artist and title. An unusual approach to art appreciation.

Wick, Walter. *Can You See What I See? Treasure Ship.* Scholastic, 2010. Ages 4–7. A seek and find book with marvelous illustrations.

Winter, Jonah. *Dizzy.* Illustrated by Sean Qualls. Arthur A. Levine Books, 2006. Ages 6–8. The story of musician, Dizzy Gillespie, who broke the rules of music to create a unique sound.

Winter, Jonah. *The 39 Apartments of Ludwig Van Beethoven.* Illustrated by Barry Blitt. Schwartz & Wade Books, 2006. Ages 6–8. The tale of how Beethoven's legless pianos were moved out of one apartment to the next, and the next, and the next while he continued to compose.

Yolen, Jane. *Apple for the Teacher.* Abrams, 2005. Ages 6–10. Thirty songs for singing while you work, accompanied by works of art.

Biography

Adler, David, and Michael Adler. *A Picture Book of Dolley and James Madison.* Holiday House, 2009. Ages 6–8. A picture book biography of the president and his wife, who always had the public good at heart.

Berne, Jennifer. *Manfish: A Story of Jacques Cousteau.* Illustrated by Eric Puybaret. Chronicle Books, 2008. Ages 5–8. The little boy who fell in love with the sea and wanted to swim like the fish grew up to be Jacques Cousteau, champion of the seas. A charming biography.

Brown, Don. *Teddie.* Houghton Mifflin, 2009. Ages 5–8. The story of young Teddy Roosevelt.

Brown, Don. *Young Albert Einstein.* Houghton Mifflin, 2004. Ages 6–8. Albert was an odd child and no one would have predicted that he would become one of the world's greatest thinkers. Here is the story of that boyhood.

Brown, Tami. *Soar, Eleanor.* Illustrated by Francois Roca. Scholastic, 2010. Ages 6–8. True story of the youngest licensed U.S. pilot.

Corey, Shana. *You Forgot Your Skirt, Amelia Bloomer!* Illustrated by Chesley McLaren. Scholastic, 2000. Ages 6–8. The true story of a woman who fought injustice and skirted conventions by designing an outfit for herself with a skirt and pants, quite shocking for her day. Not only did she change clothing styles but she struck a blow as well for women's rights.

Chandra, Deborah, and Madeleine, Comora. *George Washington's Teeth.* Illustrated by Brock Cole. Ages 5–7. George Washington suffered all his life with tooth problems and when elected president he had only two teeth left.

Clinton, Catherine. *Phillis's Big Test.* Illustrated by Jean Qualls. Houghton Mifflin, 2008. Ages 6–8. In 1773 Phillis Wheatley, a slave, published a book of poetry. She was required to take a test to prove that the poems were hers. No one wanted to believe the truth, that an African girl was the author of such fine poetry.

Cook, Michelle. *Our Children Can Soar.* Bloomsbury, 2009. Ages 5–8. A celebration of Rosa Parks, Barack Obama and the pioneers of change.

Cummins, Julie. *Sam Patch, Daredevil Jumper.* Illustrated by Michael Austin. Holiday House, 2009. Ages 5–7. Sam Patch attracted his biggest crowd when he did his biggest jump into Niagara Falls in 1829!

Davies, Jacqueline. *The Boy Who Drew Birds.* Illustrated by Melissa Sweet. Houghton Mifflin, 2004. Ages 6–8. A well written easy to read biography of John James Audubon, with illustrations that help tell his story.

Farmer, Nancy. *Casey Jones's Fireman: The Story of Sim Webb.* Pictures by James Bernardin. Phyllis Fogelman Books, 1998. Ages 6–8. A fireman shovels coal into a red-hot furnace and makes sure water flows into the boiler. A mistake can mean the boiler explodes. Webb Sims, Casey Jones' fireman didn't make mistakes. Webb and Casey Jones were real people and here is one tale of why Casey's train crashed.

Giovanni, Mikki. *Rosa.* Illustrated by Bryan Collier. Holt, 2005. Ages 6–8. A beautifully illustrated biography of Rosa Parks.

Hesse, Karen. *The Young Hans Christian Andersen.* Illustrated by Erik Blegvad. Scholastic, 2005. Ages 6–8. An intimate and gripping biography of the early life of the famed storyteller. Highly recommended.

High, Linda Oatman. *The Girl on the High-Diving Horse.* Illustrated by Ted Lewin. Philomel, 2003. Ages 6–8. In Atlantic City in 1930 Cordelia goes daily to see the girl on the high-diving horse. Is it possible that she, too, might someday be that girl?

Hopkinson, Deborah. *Keep On!* Illustrated by Stephen Alcorn. Peachtree, 2009. The story of explorer Mathew Henson, codiscoverer of the North Pole. Ages 6–8.

Kerley, Barbara. *What to Do About Alice?* Illustrated by Edwin Cunningham. Scholastic, 2008. Ages 6–8. A lively biography of Alice Roosevelt, oldest daughter of President Theodore Roosevelt.

Kimmelman, Leslie. *Mind Your Manners, Alice Roosevelt.* Illustrated by Adam Gustavson. Peachtree, 2009. Ages 6–8. True events in the lives of Theodore Roosevelt and his daughter Alice.

Kramer, S.A. *Night Flight: Charles Lindbergh's Incredible Adventure.* Grosset & Dunlap, 2011. Ages 4–6. An easy to read account of this famous flight.

Krensky, Stephen. *Shooting for the Moon.* Illustrated by Bernie Fuchs. Farrar, 2001. Ages 5–7. A lively yet easy to read biography of Annie Oakley, from her childhood of poverty on a hardscrabble Ohio farm, hired out to a couple so mean she calls them "The Wolves," to her fame as a sharpshooter in Buffalo Bill's Wild West Show.

Krull, Kathleen, and Paul Brewer. *Lincoln Tells a Joke.* Illustrated by Stacy Innerst. Harcourt, 2010. Ages 6–8. A very readable picture book biography — how laughter saved the president and the country.

Lorbiecki, Marybeth. *Jackie's Bat.* Illustrated by Brian Pinkney. Simon & Schuster, 2006. Ages 6–8. A fictionalized account of how Jackie Robinson broke through professional baseball's color barrier.

Mazer, Harry. *My Brother Abe.* Simon & Schuster, 2009. Ages 6–8. Sally Lincoln tells what it was like to be Abraham's sister.

McCully, Emily Arnold. *The Escape of Oney Judge.* Farrar, 2007. Ages 6–8. Martha Washington's slave escapes to freedom.

McCully, Emily Arnold. *Marvelous Mattie.* Farrar, 2006. Ages 6–8. Based on the life of inventor Margaret E. Knight, the story of how she won a patent for her paper bag machine at a time when women were not supposed to be inventors.

Moses, Will. *Johnny Appleseed: The Story of a Legend.* Philomel, 2001. Ages 5–7. Will Moses uses folk art to follow the real-life Johnny, the apple tree planting folk hero who helped open and tame the American frontier.

Nelson, S.D. *Quiet Hero.* Lee & Low Books, 2006. Ages 6–8. The story of Native American Ira Hayes, one of the flag raisers on Iwo Jima in World War II.

Noyes, Deborah. *When I Met the Wolf Girls.* Illustrated by August Hall. Houghton Mifflin, 2007. Ages 6–8. A slightly fictionalized account of two girls raised by wolves and brought to civilization.

Rabin, Staton. *Mr. Lincoln's Boys.* Illustrated by Bagram Ibatoulline. Viking, 2008. Ages 6–8.

Rockwell, Anne. *Big George*. Illustrated by Matt Phelan. Harcourt, 2009. Ages 6–8. How a shy, hot-tempered boy became President Washington.

Rockwell, Ann. *They Called Her Molly Pitcher*. Knopf, 2002. Ages 6–8. A rousing tale of the American Revolution and one very independent-minded woman, Molly Pitcher.

Sullivan, George. *Helen Keller: Her Life in Pictures*. Scholastic, 2007. Ages 6–8. A breathtaking collection of photographs that highlight the life of this famous woman.

Taylor, Gaylia. *George Crum and the Saratoga Chip*. Illustrated by Frank Morrison. Lee & Low Books, 2006. Ages 6–8. In reacting to a diner who sent back his potatoes, George, a cook, made potatoes so thin and crisp that he is considered the inventor of the potato chip. Fun illustrations for this true story.

U'Ren. *Mary Smith*. Farrar, 2003. Ages 5–7. The true story of a woman whose job it was to wake up the people of her town by shooting pebbles at their windows.

Wallner, Alexandra. *Lucy Maud Montgomery*. Holiday House, 2006. Ages 6–8. A picture book biography of the author of *Anne of Green Gables*.

Social Studies

Appelt, Kathi. *Miss Lady Bird's Wildflowers*. Illustrated by Joy Hein. Boyds Mill, 2005. Ages 5–8. The story of how Lady Bird Johnson, the First Lady, helped to beautify America.

Atwell, Debby. *Pearl*. Houghton Mifflin, 2001. Ages 6–8. A little girl named Pearl takes readers on a journey through the history of the United States as she recounts her family's ups and downs, each moment accented by a historical landmark, from the hardships of the Civil War to the Wright brothers' first flight to the Great Depression and eventually to the first walk on the moon.

Banks, Kate. *A Gift from the Sea*. Illustrated by Georg Hallensleben. Farrar, 2001. Ages 6–8. When the boy found the rock, he did not know that it had made a journey through time to reach him. From the beginning of time through the earliest civilizations to the present day, here is a simply told history of the Earth for young students.

Barretta, Gene. *Now and Ben*. Henry Holt, 2006. Ages 4–6. Cleverly illustrated, the modern inventions of Benjamin Franklin!

Beccia, Carlyn. *Who Put the B in the Ballyhoo?* Houghton Mifflin, 2007. Ages 6–8. An ABC introduction to bizarre and celebrated circus performers.

Brown, Craig. *Barn Raising*. Greenwillow, 2002. Ages 5–7. An Amish community builds a barn in a day. A tale of generosity, cooperation and neighborly concern.

Brown, Don. *Dolley Madison Saves George Washington*. Houghton Mifflin, 2007. Ages 6–8. How Dolley saved the White House treasures when the British attacked.

Cole Joanna. *Mrs. Frizzle's Adventures in Ancient Egypt*. Illustrated by Bruce Degen. Scholastic, 2001. Ages 6–8. Mrs. Frizzle and her tour group parachute into the past, where they help build a pyramid and see the making of a mummy.

Cole, Joanna. *Mrs. Frizzle's Adventures: Medieval Castle*. Illustrated by Bruce Degen. Scholastic, 2003. Ages 6–8. A lavishly illustrated introduction to castles and Medieval life.

Crew, Gary. *Pig on the* Titanic. Illustrated by Bruce Whatley. HarperCollins, 2005. Ages 5–7. The true story of how a small musical pig calmed the fears of children in a lifeboat after the sinking of the *Titanic*.

Deedy, Carmen Agra. *Fourteen Cows for America*. Illustrated by Thomas Gonzalez. Peachtree, 2009. Ages 6–8. The true tale of a gift from the Masai of Kenya to the people of the U.S. to show their compassion for the losses of 9/11.

Dennis, Brian. *Nubs*. Little, Brown, 2009. Ages 6–8. The true story of a mutt, a marine and a miracle.

Drummond, Allan. *Liberty!* Farrar, 2002. Ages 6–8. The story of the Statue of Liberty, from its construction in France to its unveiling on October 28, 1886.

Edwards, Pamela Duncan. *The Bus Ride That Changed History*. Illustrated by Danny Shanahan. Houghton Mifflin, 2005. Ages 5–8. The story of Rosa Parks and her refusal to give up her bus seat, an act which changed the course of American history.

Fearrington, Ann. *Who Sees the Lighthouse?* Illustrated by Giles Laroche. Ages 4–6. A counting book in which all manner of creatures are drawn to the beacons of lighthouses. Bold, dramatic illustrations.

Geisert, Bonnie and Arthur Geisert. *Desert Town*. Houghton Mifflin, 2001. Ages 6–8. A desert town, once the end of the line for shipping cattle, is no longer a stopping point for the railroad. The town endures blazing heat throughout the summer months, and everyone must find a way to stay cool. Some do their work at night, some take refuge in an air-conditioned store and everyone moves at a slow pace. The wonder and personality of everyday life in a small town.

Griffin, Kitty. *The Ride*. Illustrated by Marjorie Priceman. Scholastic, 2010. Ages 6–8. True tale of a Colonial heroine who made a famous ride.

Harrison, David. *Pirates*. Wordsong, 2008. Ages 6–8. Poems that tell of thugs, misfits, high points and low points in the life of a pirate!

Harrison, David L. *Rivers: Nature's Wondrous Waterways*. Illustrated by Cheryl Nathan. Ages 6–8. Readers are taken on a journey down a river from its source at the top of a mountain to its mouth where it meets the sea. Beautiful poetic language!

Hartland, Jessie. *Night Shift*. Bloomsbury, 2008. Ages 5–7. Discover the world of work that goes on at night.

Johnson, Angela. *Those Building Men*. Illustrated by Barry Moser. Blue Sky Press, 2001. Ages 5–7. A simple, dramatic tribute to the men who gave their strength, sweat, courage and vision to the building of America's bridges, railroads and skyscrapers.

Kelly, Irene. *A Small Dog's Big Life*. Holiday House, 2005. Ages 5–7. The true story of the stray dog, Owney, who became a world traveler.

Kennedy, Edward M. *My Senator and Me: A Dog's Eye View of Washington, D.C.* Scholastic, 2006. Ages 5–8. A day with a United States senator and his dog is a great introduction for primary children to the work of our lawmakers.

Krensky, Stephen. *Paul Revere's Midnight Ride*. Illustrated by Greg Harlin. HarperCollins, 2002. Ages 6–8. A dramatic account of the night Paul Revere galloped into history.

Leedy, Loreen. *Follow the Money*. Holiday House, 2002. Ages 5–7. The travels of George, a quarter, from the time he is minted to his return to the bank.

Levine, Ellen. *Henry's Freedom Box*. Illustrated by Kadir Nelson. Scholastic, 2007. Ages 5–7. Henry, a young slave, mails himself to freedom.

McCarthy, Meghan. *Aliens Are Coming!* Knopf, 2006. Ages 6–8. The true account of the 1938 War of the Worlds radio broadcast.

McCully, Emily. *The Secret Cave*. Farrar, 2010. Ages 6–8. The true tale of four French boys who discovered more than 2000 paintings in a cave at Lascaux. The paintings were more than 17,000 years old.

McCully, Emily. *Wonder Horse*. Holt 2010. Ages 6–9. A beautifully illustrated, well written account of the world's smartest horse.

McDonald, Megan. *Saving the Liberty Bell*. Illustrated by Marsha Gray Carrington. Atheneum, 2005. Ages 6–8. A lively telling of the hiding of the Liberty Bell under church floorboards when the Redcoats were coming.

Melmed, Laura K. *Capital!* Illustrated by Frane Lessac. HarperCollins, 2003. Ages 6–8. Washington, D.C., from A to Z. Colorfully illustrated.

Michelson, Richard. *Tuttle's Red Barn*. Illustrated by Mary Azarian. G.P. Putnam's Sons, 2007. Ages 4–6. American history recounted through twelve generations of a family on a real farm.

Miller, Dennis. *Big Alaska*. Illustrated by Jon Van Zyle. Walker, 2006. Ages 6–8. A picture book journey across America's most amazing state. Lively text and magnificent illustrations.

Nobisso, Josephine. *John Blair and the Great Hinckley Fire*. Illustrated by Ted

Rose. Houghton Mifflin, 2000. Ages 5–8. In 1894 amidst flames of the most devastating firestorm in the U.S., John Blair, the train porter, acted with courage and compassion. Here is the untold story of a hero history almost forgot.

St. George, Judith. *So You Want to Be an Inventor.* Illustrated by David Small. Philomel, 2002. Ages 6–9. A humorous look at a variety of inventors and their similarities and differences.

Schanzer, Rosalyn. *How Ben Franklin Stole the Lightning.* HarperCollins, 2003. Ages 6–8. Find Ben Franklin busy at work on every spread and discover how he found a way to steal the lightning right out of the sky.

Schulevitz, Uri. *How I Learned Geography.* Farrar, Straus & Giroux, 2008. Ages 5–9. The author/artist recalls his childhood in World War II and the map that took him far away from his hunger and misery.

Shea, Pegi. *Liberty Rising.* Illustrated by Wade Zahares. Henry Holt, 2005. Ages 6–8. The story of the Statue of Liberty told with magnificent, bold illustrations.

Sills, Leslie. *From Rags to Riches.* Holiday House, 2005. Ages 6–8. An illustrated history of girls' clothing in America.

Simon, Seymour. *Seymour Simon's Book of Trains.* HarperCollins, 2002. Ages 4–6. Different trains and their uses illustrated with full color photographs.

Spradlin, Michael. *Daniel Boone's Great Escape.* Illustrated by Ard Hoyt. Walker, 2008. Ages 5–7. A true account of Boone's escape from the Shawnee and his four-day journey over 180 miles to warn the settlers of an attack.

Stevenson, Harvey. *Looking at Liberty.* HarperCollins, 2003. Ages 6–8. The story of the Statue of Liberty told through verse and paintings.

Takabayashi, Mari. *I Live in Tokyo.* Houghton Mifflin, 2001. Ages 4–7. A brightly illustrated introduction to a year in Tokyo, including food, transportation, celebrations, buildings, activities and more.

Talbott, Hudson. *United Tweets of America.* G.P. Putnam's Sons, 2008. Ages 6–8. Birds and their home states come to life with energy and humor.

Van Rynbach, Iris, and Pegi Shea. *The Taxing Case of the Cows.* Illustrated by Emily McCully. Clarion Books, 2010. Ages 6–8. A true account of the Smith sisters, who, in 1869, refused to pay a tax on their farm since they were not allowed to vote. Short accounts of fourteen people who risked their lives for peace.

Waters, Kate. *Giving Thanks.* The 1621 harvest feast. Scholastic, 2001. Ages 4–6. The first Thanksgiving feast beautifully recreated in photographs.

Woodruff, Elvira. *Small Beauties.* Illustrated by Adam Rex. Knopf, 2006. Ages 6–8. Darcy O'Hara sees small beauties all around her, even when her family is forced to leave Ireland for America.

Yaccarino, Dan. *Go, Go America*. Scholastic Press, 2008. Ages 6–10. Fun facts and illustrations about each state.
Yolen, Jane. *Naming Liberty*. Illustrated by Jim Burke. Philomel, 2008. Ages 6–8. The story of the building of the Statue of Liberty.

Science

Arnosky, Jim. *Turtle in the Sea*. G.P. Putnam's Sons, 2002. Ages 4–6. Turtle must battle sharks, boats, storms and nets to stay alive. An exciting tale.
Aston, Dianna, and Sylvia Long. *A Seed Is Sleepy*. Chronicle Books, 2007. Ages 4–6. Beautifully illustrated introduction to many kinds of seeds.
Bauer, Marion Dane. *A Bear Named Trouble*. Clarion, 2005. Ages 6–8. A boy and a bear part ways when the bear kills the zoo's Mama Goose. A story told from two points of view.
Bishop, Nic. *Backyard Detective: Critters Up Close*. Scholastic, 2002. Ages 6–8. A photographic exploration of creatures common to backyards. Young explorers will discover their own miniature wilderness.
Bond, Rebecca. *In The Belly of an Ox*. Houghton Mifflin, 2009. Ages 6–8. The unexpected photographic adventures of Richard and Cherry Kearton.
Bowen, Betsy. *Gathering: A Northwoods Counting Book*. Houghton Mifflin, 1999. Ages 5–7. The Northwoods is "one seed, two rhubarb pies, four bears, five blueberries"—all the things associated with this area of the country. Find ten things associated with your city, state, province or country.
Bradley, Kimberly B. *Energy Makes Things Happen*. Illustrated by Paul Meisel. HarperCollins, 2002. Ages 6–8. An excellent introduction to energy shows how energy makes things happen on land, in water and in the sky.
Cole, Henry. *On the Way to the Beach*. Greenwillow, 2003. Ages 4–6. Find a place to sit and watch and listen. On the beach or in the woods or in a salt marsh, what can you see and hear?
Dope, Sam. *Gotta Go! Gotta Go!* Illustrated by Sue Riddle. Farrar, 2000. Ages 6–8. A bug know that she's gotta go to Mexico and makes the impossible journey, as the Monarch butterflies do each year when they migrate from Canada to the mountains of Mexico.
Duke, Kate. *Twenty Is Too Many*. Dutton, 2000. Ages 4–6. A clever introduction to subtraction as one boat is too small to hold twenty guinea pigs.
Duquette, Keith. *They Call Me Woolly*. G.P. Putnam's Sons, 2002. Ages 5–7. Striking illustrations and simple text show a variety of animals and tell how they got their names.
Florian, Douglas. *Comets, Stars, the Moon and Mars*. Harcourt, 2007. Ages 6–8. Delightful space poems and paintings.

Fraser, Mary Ann. *How Animal Babies Stay Safe*. HarperCollins, 2002. Ages 5–7. Some animal babies depend on their parents. Some help each other. Some manage on their own. But all must find a way to keep safe.

George, Jean Craighead. *The Wolves Are Back*. Illustrated by Wenall Minor. Dutton, 2008. Ages 6–8. How wolves were brought back from near extinction.

Gerstein, Mordicai. *Sparrow Jack*. Farrar, 2003. Ages 6–8. A true tale of how sparrows came to America to solve the inchworm problem in Philadelphia.

Gibbons, Gail. *Apples*. Holiday House, 2000 Ages 4–6. Information, brightly illustrated, about how apple trees grow, their various parts and the different varieties. Instructions on how to plant and care for an apple tree are included.

Gibbons, Gail. *Tornadoes!* Holiday House, 2009. Ages 6–8. An easy to read introduction to tornadoes with vibrant illustrations.

Goldish, Meish. *Bug-A-Licious*. Bearport, 2009. Ages 6–8. People do eat grasshopper tacos and buggy pizza and all are displayed here in full color with a lively text.

Goldish, Meish. *Titanic Trucks*. Bearport, 2009. Ages 4–6. One of a series that includes airplanes, roller coasters and earth movers. Simply written with excellent photographs, with bibliography, glossary and index.

High, Linda Oatman. *City of Snow: The Great Blizzard of 1888*. Illustrated by Laura Francesca Filippucci. Walker, 2004. Ages 6–9. Haunting illustrations and free verse narration bring the blizzard alive, showing the hardships when the largest city in the country was shut down.

Hort, Lenny. *Did Dinosaurs Eat Pizza?* Illustrated by John O'Brien. Henry Holt, 2006. Ages 6–8. Mysteries about dinosaurs that science hasn't solved.

Jenkins, Steve. *Down Down Down*. Houghton Mifflin, 2009. Ages 4–8. Travel to the bottom of the sea and see the mysterious creatures that live there.

Jenkins, Steve. *Never Smile at a Monkey*. Houghton Mifflin, 2009. Ages 5–10. Information about 17 dangerous animals.

Jenkins, Steve, and Robin Page. *What Do You Do with a Tail Like This?* Houghton Mifflin, 2003. Ages 4–7. Animal parts are shown on one page and the animals and how they use them on the next.

Jeppson, Ann-Sofie. *Here Comes Pontus!* Illustrated by Catarina Kruusval. R & S Books, 2000. Ages 4–7. As a young colt goes to live on a farm with a human family, readers learn about feeding, equipment and care of horses. An excellent introduction for young horse lovers.

Lach, William. *My Friends the Flowers*. Illustrated by Doug Kennedy. Abrams, 2010. Ages 4–7. A beautifully illustrated rhyming introduction to the world of flowers.

Larson, Kirby, and Mary Nethery. *Two Bobbies*. Illustrated by Jean Cassels.

Walker, 2008. Ages 6–8. A true story of Hurricane Katrina, friendship and survival.

Ledwon, Peter, and Marilyn Mets. *Midnight Math*. Holiday House, 2000. Ages 6–8. Animals have fun with twelve terrific math games shown in comic book style with step-by-step directions. Good for improving skills in addition, subtraction and multiplication.

Lee, Milly. *Earthquake*. Illustrated by Yangsook Choi. Farrar, 2001. Ages 6–8. In 1906 in San Francisco, the earth shook. Buildings fell. Fires flared and hundreds fled their homes, as did Milly Lee's mother. A true account of the devastating San Francisco earthquake.

Lerner, Carol. *Butterflies in the Garden*. HarperCollins, 2002. Ages 5–7. A beautifully illustrated introduction to butterflies and how to lure them into your garden.

Ljungkvist, Laura, *Follow the Line Around the World*. Viking, 2008. Ages 4–7. Learn about animals and their habitats all around the world.

Lunis, Natalie. *Dachshund: The Hot Dogger*. Bearport, 2009. Ages 4–8. Lively text and photographs give considerable information about this dog.

Lunis, Natalie. *Green Iguanas*. Bearport, 2009. Ages 6–8. One of a series that includes Furry Ferrets, Miniature Horses and Potbellied Pigs. Simply written with excellent photographs with bibliography, glossary and index.

Lunis, Natalie. *Portuguese Man of War: Floating Misery*. Bearport, 2009. Ages 6–8. One of a series that includes the shark, eel, stonefish, etc. Simply written with excellent photographs, with bibliography, glossary and index. Vacation poems that cover everything from the hotel ice machine to filling brothers' shorts with sand! A sure winner!

McCarthy, Meghan. *Seabiscuit, Wonder Horse*. Simon & Schuster, 2008. Ages 4–7. An outstanding true tale of the famous racehorse, of hope and determination and belief in the unbelievable. An outstanding book!

McNulty, Faith. *If You Decide to Go to the Moon*. Illustrated by Steven Kellogg. Scholastic, 2005. Ages 5–8. An imaginary journey to discover the moon told in elegant and informative prose with delightful and playful illustrations.

Miller, David. *Just Like You and Me*. Dial, 2001. Ages 4–7. "Do you race like a cheetah, huddle like a penguin, dance like a crane?" People and animals are alike in all sorts of ways though sometimes we may seem to be very different. Here is a book of simple yet funny and apt comparisons.

Morrison, Taylor. *Tsunami Warning*. Houghton Mifflin, 2007. Ages 6–8. Learn what a tsunami is like through the eyes of those who lived through one. Magnificent illustrations.

Nez, John Abbott. *Cromwell Dixon's Sky-Cycle*. G.P. Putnam's Sons, 2009. Ages 6–8. In 1907, Cromwell Dixon, with the help of his mother, designed, built and flew a flying bicycle!

Patten, Brian. *The Blue-Green Ark*. An Alphabet for Planet Earth. Scholastic, 2000. Ages 6–8. "A is for Ark. For the blue and green Ark adrift in the dark." So begins this alphabet where each letter celebrates the many natural wonders of the world, from the Earth' s smallest creatures to the vast night skies above us.

Sayre, April. *Crocodile Listens*. Illustrated by JoEllen Stammen. Greenwillow, 2001. Ages 5–7. A tasty frog croaks. Delicious warthogs tramp by. Crocodile doesn't move. She hasn't eaten in weeks. But she only lies and listens. Crocodile has a secret hidden in the sand.

Simon, Seymour. *Animals Nobody Loves*. Sea Star, 2001. Ages 6–8. From the deadly black widow spider to a twenty-five foot long man-eating crocodile.

Stewart, Melissa. *A Place for Birds*. Illustrated by Higgins Bond. Peachtree, 2009. Ages 6–8. Ways human action or inaction can affect birds.

Stewart, Melissa. *Under the Snow*. Illustrated by Constance Bergum. Peachtree, 2009. Ages 4–7. Animals as they live out the winter through snow and ice.

Tang, Greg. *The Grapes of Math*. Illustrated by Harry Briggs. Scholastic, 2001. Ages 6–8. Math puzzles that can be solved by using a few simple but effective techniques.

Tang, Greg. *Math Appeal*. Illustrated by Harry Briggs. Scholastic, 2003. Ages 4–7. Each clever riddle poses a problem and offers a helpful hint to the solution.

Waldman, Neil. *The Never-Ending Greenness*. Boyds Mill, 2003. Ages 6–8. The story of the Jews who escape to Israel and build a new home.

Waters, Kate. *Mary Geddy's Day*. Photographs by Russ Kendall. Scholastic, 1999. Ages 4–7. The latest addition to this popular series follows a colonial girl through a day in Williamsburg.

Wethered, Peggy, and Ken Edgett. *Touchdown Mars!* Illustrated by Michael Chesworth. G.P. Putnam's Sons, 2000. Ages 4–7. An alphabet adventure that reveals interesting facts about Mars and space travel and what you might find on a trip beyond the stratosphere.

Zoehfeld, Kathleen Weidner. *Dinosaurs Big and Small*. HarperCollins, 2002. Ages 4–7. Colorful illustrations of favorite creatures.

Index